혼공

기초영문법

혼공 허준석 지음

L3

혼공 기초 영문법 Level 3

1판 1쇄 2022년 2월 7일
1판 4쇄 2024년 4월 1일

지은이 허준석
표지디자인 박새롬
내지디자인 황지영
표지그림 김효지
마케팅 두잉글 사업 본부
브랜드 혼공북스
펴낸곳 혼공북스
출판등록 제2021-000288호
주　소 04033 서울특별시 마포구 양화로 113 4층(서교동)
전자메일 team@hongong.co.kr

ISBN　979-11-976810-5-9　13740

혼공!

영어 공부 참 어렵습니다. 특히, 영문법이란 말을 들으면 어디서부터 시작해야 할지 앞이 깜깜합니다. 저 역시도 그러한 경험을 했었기에, 세상에서 가장 쉽게 영문법 공부를 할 수 있는 책이나 강의가 있으면 좋겠다고 생각을 했습니다. 그래서, 혼공 기초 영문법이 탄생했습니다. 짧은 이론, 반복되는 개념, 쓰기 위주의 연습을 통해 그 동안 공부해오던 공부 방식을 벗어날 수 있을 것입니다.

영문법에는 규칙도 많고, 예외도 참 많습니다. 많은 사람들은 예외를 보면서 겁에 질려 영어 공부를 중단하게 됩니다. 그럴 필요 없습니다. 왜 규칙이 생겼는지 이해하고, 조금 외우고, 예외는 이런 게 있구나 하고 넘어가도 됩니다. 이렇게 반복해서 학습하다보면 애쓰지 않아도 예외까지 완벽하게 익혀지게 됩니다. 반대로, 처음부터 예외를 파고들어 공부한다면, 실수할까봐 영어로 말하기도 쓰기도 제대로 못하게 됩니다.

혼공 영어는 결국 말하고, 실전에서 쓸 수 있는 영어를 목표로 하고 있습니다. 쉽게 공부해서 자신감을 찾고, 짐짐 더 깊이 있는 공부를 하면서 내가 원하는 영어 실력에 도달하길 바랍니다. 재미있게 끝까지 간다면 무조건 성공합니다. 끈기를 가지고 혼공하세요!

혼공 허준석 드림

오리엔테이션

1 단어

8품사(명사, 대명사, 동사, 형용사, 부사, 전치사, 접속사, 감탄사)에 해당하는 하나 하나의 조각을 말합니다.

> 예 Jason(명사), him(대명사), run(동사), handsome(형용사), slowly(부사), at(전치사),
> and(접속사), hooray(감탄사)

2 구

상대방에게 좀 더 자세한 정보를 주기 위해 두 개 이상의 단어가 모여 하나의 문법 요소가 되는 것을 말합니다.

> 예 in the park(전치사구), the man(명사구), the man on the stage(명사구)...

3 절(문장)

주어(동작의 주인)와 술어(동작이 담긴 부분)가 모두 있는 것을 절(문장)이라고 합니다.

> 예 The man on the stage / played the piano.
>
> (주어: 무대에 있는 그 남자는, 술어: 피아노를 연주했다)

4 핵

구에서는 반드시 의미의 핵심이 되는 부분이 존재합니다. 명사구와 동사구에서 핵을 잘 파악해야 문장을 쉽게 이해할 수 있습니다.

> 예 the man on the stage(핵: man)
>
> played the piano(핵: played)

🔎 혼공개념　문장이 길어지는 원리

1 단계

하나의 주어 + 술어로 문장을 이룹니다.

> 예) The man on the stage / played the piano.
> 　　주어　　　　　　　　　　　　술어

2 단계

하나의 문장 속의 '일부분'으로 접속사가 이끄는 하나의 문장을 집어넣습니다.

> 예) The man on the stage / said that he loved us.
> 　　주어　　　　　　　　　　　　술어

3 단계

다양한 접속사로 문장과 문장을 연결합니다.

> 예) The man on the stage played the piano, / and I really liked it.
> 　　　　　　문장 1　　　　　　　　　　　　　　문장 2

> The man on the stage played the piano, / and I thought that you would like this.
> 　　　　　　문장 1　　　　　　　　　　　　　　　　　문장 2

> When I was young, / I didn't like English.
> 　　문장 1　　　　　　　문장 2

contents

혼공 기초 영문법

LEVEL 3

혼공 기초 영문법
LEVEL 3

to부정사 심화 1

혼공개념 의미상의 주어란?

1 의미상의 주어: to부정사에 나오는 '동작'의 주인

> 예 It is difficult <u>to concentrate</u> in the morning.
>
> It is difficult for Jun <u>to concentrate</u> in the morning.
>
> The box is too heavy <u>to carry</u>.
>
> The box is too heavy for her <u>to carry</u>.

혼공개념 의미상의 주어의 종류

1 앞에 나온 형용사가 일의 성격을 나타낼 때: for + 목적격

> 예 It was <u>impossible</u> for him to work with his father.

2 앞에 나온 형용사가 사람의 성격을 나타낼 때: of + 목적격

> 예 It is so <u>nice</u> of them <u>to say</u> so.

혼공 팁

의미상의 주어를 쓸 때, for인지 of인지를 판단하기 위해서는 주어 자리로 이동시켜보자.

> 예 He was impossible to work with his father. (X)
>
> They are so nice to say so. (O)

일의 성격을 나타내는 형용사		사람의 성격을 나타내는 형용사	
hard		nice	
difficult		kind	
possible	for + 목적격	polite	of + 목적격
impossible		foolish	
important		careless	
dangerous		rude	

A 다음 문장에 들어갈 의미상의 주어를 빈칸에 쓴 뒤, 들어갈 알맞은 위치에 V 표시하시오.

① It is very difficult to concentrate in the morning.

_____ (Jun)

② The box is too heavy to carry.

_____ (she)

③ It was impossible to work with his father.

_____ (he)

④ It is so nice to say so.

_____ (they)

β 다음 <보기> 안에 있는 형용사를 알맞은 곳에 위치시키시오.

| <보기>   hard nice difficult kind brave possible polite |
| impossible foolish important careless dangerous rude stupid |

일의 성격을 나타내는 형용사		사람의 성격을 나타내는 형용사	
	for + 목적격		of + 목적격

A 다음 괄호 안에서 어법상 알맞은 것을 고르시오.

① It was very kind (of / for) the students to help the homeless.

② It was so stupid (of / for) Mike to do that.

③ It is so careless (of / for) him to get there by car.

④ It is dangerous (of / for) Melanie to go out by herself.

B 다음 문장의 빈칸에 들어갈 의미상의 주어를 완성하시오.

① It is dangerous _____ to climb that mountain in this weather. (he)

② It was very polite _____ to see me off. (they)

③ It is important _____ to have a dream. (we)

C 우리말 의미와 일치하도록 주어진 단어들을 올바르게 배열하시오.

① 그의 수업은 내가 이해하기에 어려웠다.

(difficult / me / his / understand / was / class / for / to / it)

_____

② Jun이 이 수학 문제를 푸는 것은 쉽다.

(Jun / math / it / for / to / solve / is / this / easy / problem)

_____

A. 다음 <보기> 안에 있는 형용사를 알맞은 곳에 위치시키시오.

<보기>	hard	nice	difficult	kind	brave	possible	polite
	impossible	foolish	important	careless	dangerous	rude	stupid

일의 성격을 나타내는 형용사		사람의 성격을 나타내는 형용사	
	for + 목적격		of + 목적격

B. 다음 문장들을 우리말로 해석하시오.

① It is very difficult for Jun to concentrate in the morning.

_____

② It was very kind of the students to help the homeless.

_____

③ It is so careless of him to get there by car.

_____

④ It is dangerous for him to climb that mountain in this weather.

_____

to부정사 심화 2

💡 **혼공개념** to부정사의 부정

1 방법: to부정사의 앞에 not이나 never을 써서 부정함

예 He decided not(never) <u>to go</u> on a business trip.

My mom told me not(never) <u>to be</u> late again.

혼공 팁

to부정사를 부정할 때와 문장의 동사를 부정할 때는 서로 의미가 다르니 주의하자.

예 My mom didn't tell me to be late again.

💡 **혼공개념** 대부정사란?

1 대부정사: 앞에서 이미 나온 to부정사를 다시 쓸 때 to만 쓸 수 있는 것을 말함

예 A: Hey, you don't have to go now.

B: I don't want to (go now), but it's already 11 p.m.

💡 **혼공개념** to부정사의 부사적 용법

1 명사적 용법, 형용사적 용법 외에 다양하게 쓰이는 용법

1) 목적(~하기 위해): I stayed up all night <u>to study</u> math.

2) 감정의 원인(~해서): I'm very surprised <u>to hear</u> the news.

3) 판단의 근거(~하다니): He is very kind <u>to help</u> the poor.

4) 형용사 수식(~하기에): His chair is comfortable <u>to sit on</u>.

5) 결과(그 결과 ~하다): The shy boy grew up <u>to be</u> an actor.

혼공 연습

 다음 문장에서 to부정사를 찾아 밑줄을 긋고, 부정하기 위해 not(never)을 쓸 위치에 V 표시하시오.

① He decided to go on a business trip.

② My mom told me to be late again.

③ My brother told me to turn off the TV.

④ Kevin's mom told Kevin to leave the water running.

 다음 문장에서 밑줄 친 부분을 우리말로 옮기시오.

① I stayed up all night to study math.

_____

② I'm very sad to hear that.

_____

③ He is very kind to help the poor.

_____

④ His chair is comfortable to sit on.

_____

⑤ The shy boy grew up to be an actor.

_____

A 다음 <보기>와 같이 to부정사를 사용하여 한 문장으로 만드시오.

> <보기>　　　　　He told me. + Don't touch his stuff.
> ⇒ He told me not to touch his stuff.

① My sister told me. + Don't wear her clothes.

_____

② My mom wanted me. + Don't play computer games too often.

_____

③ Jason advised us. + Don't walk around while we eat.

_____

B 다음 밑줄 친 to 뒤에 생략된 내용을 찾아 밑줄을 그으시오.

① A: Would you like to have some coffee?
　　B: Yes, I'd like <u>to</u>.

② A: You can call Mr. Kim if you'd like <u>to</u>.

C 다음 문장에서 밑줄 친 부분을 우리말로 옮기시오.

① She grew up <u>to be famous</u>.　　_____

② I eat little <u>to lose weight</u>.　　_____

③ These pants are small <u>to wear</u>.　　_____

A. 다음 문장들을 우리말로 해석하시오.

① My mom didn't tell me to be late again.

_____

② My mom told me not to be late again.

_____

B. 다음 문장 속의 to부정사를 not으로 부정하시오.

③ My brother told me to turn off the TV.

_____

④ Kevin's mom told Kevin to leave the water running.

_____

⑤ Jason advised us to walk around while we eat.

_____

C. 다음 문장들을 우리말로 해석하시오.

⑥ I stayed up all night to study math.

_____

⑦ His chair is comfortable to sit on.

_____

⑧ These pants are small to wear.

_____

정답 ① 내 엄마는 나에게 또 다시 늦으라고 말하지 않았다. ② 내 엄마는 나에게 다시는 늦지 말라고 말씀하셨다. ③ My brother told me not to turn off the TV. ④ Kevin's mom told Kevin not to leave the water running. ⑤ Jason advised us not to walk around while we eat. ⑥ 나는 수학 공부를 하기 위해 밤을 샜다. ⑦ 그의 의자는 앉기에 편하다. ⑧ 이 바지는 입기에 작다.

to부정사 심화 3

🔎 혼공개념 | be to 용법이란?

1 be to 용법: 'be동사 + to + 동사원형'으로 격식 있는 표현이며, 기본적인 조동사를 포함한 다양한 의미로 쓰임

1) 예정 : ~할 예정이다

We <u>are to visit</u> Paris next year.

2) 의무 : ~해야 한다

You <u>are to wash</u> your hands before you eat.

3) 의도 : ~하려고 한다

If we <u>are to catch</u> the train, we have to hurry up.

4) 가능 : ~할 수 있다

No one <u>was to be seen</u> in the park.

5) 운명 : ~할 운명이다

They <u>were never to see</u> their country.

혼공 팁

be to 용법과 to부정사의 명사적 용법은 비슷하게 보이지만, 의미가 다르다.

예 My dream is <u>to visit</u> Paris next year. (to부정사의 명사적 용법)

We are <u>to visit</u> Paris next year. (be to 용법)

혼공 연습

 다음 <보기>처럼 be to 용법에 밑줄을 긋고 그 부분만 우리말로 해석하시오.

<보기>　　　　　You <u>are to finish</u> the report by five.
⇒ 끝내야 한다

① If we <u>are to catch</u> the bus, we have to hurry up.

_____

② No one <u>was to be</u> seen in the park.

_____

③ They <u>were never to see</u> their country.

_____

④ You <u>are to wash</u> your hands before you eat.

_____

⑤ We <u>are to visit</u> Paris next year.

_____

B 다음 밑줄 친 to부정사가 명사적 용법인지, be to 용법에 속하는지 ○ 표시하시오.

① My job is <u>to teach</u> English. (명사적 용법 / be to 용법)

② We are <u>to respect</u> our parents. (명사적 용법 / be to 용법)

③ They are <u>to meet</u> in Danang. (명사적 용법 / be to 용법)

④ To see is <u>to believe</u>. (명사적 용법 / be to 용법)

A 두 문장의 뜻이 같도록 be to 용법을 이용하여 빈칸을 채우시오.

① You should obey the rules.

= You _____ the rules.

② They will go out for a walk after dinner.

= They _____ after dinner.

B 다음 우리말을 참고하여 주어진 표현들을 올바로 배열하시오.

① John은 Sally와 다음 달에 결혼할 예정이다.

(to / John / marry / Sally / is / next month)

_____

② 너는 그 프로젝트를 이번 금요일까지 끝내야 한다.

(are / to / by / finish / the project / you / this Friday)

_____

③ 그녀는 절대로 그녀의 가족을 다시 만나지 못할 운명이었다.

(her family / she / never / see / to / again / was)

_____

A. be to 용법에 밑줄을 긋고 그 부분만 우리말로 해석하시오.

① If we are to catch the bus, we have to hurry up.

_____

② You are to wash your hands before you eat.

_____

③ We are to visit Paris next year.

_____

④ They are to go out for a walk after dinner.

_____

B. 다음 문장들을 우리말로 해석하시오.

⑤ To see is to believe.

_____

⑥ You are to obey the rules.

_____

⑦ She was never to see her family again.

_____

정답 ① are to catch(잡으려면) ② are to wash(씻어야 한다) ③ are to visit(방문할 예정이다) ④ are to go out(나갈 예정이다) ⑤ 보는 것이 믿는 것이다. ⑥ 너는 그 규칙들을 지켜야 한다. ⑦ 그녀는 절대로 그녀의 가족을 다시 만나지 못할 운명이었다.

to부정사 심화 4

> 🔍 **혼공개념** 관용적 to부정사 구문이란?

1 to부정사와 늘 함께 쓰이는 덩어리 표현

  1) 동사 + to부정사

  예 I happened to meet her yesterday.

  He seemed to like the new song.

  2) be동사 + ~ + to부정사

  예 The show is about to begin.

  I am able to finish the job by 5 o'clock.

> 🔍 **혼공개념** 관용적 to부정사 구문

표현	우리말 뜻	표현	우리말 뜻
happen to	우연히 ~ 하다	be able to	~할 수 있다
manage to	~을 해내다	be ready to	~할 준비가 되다
seem to	~처럼 보이나	be likely to	~하기 쉽다
fail to	~을 못하게 되다	be supposed to	~하기로 되어있다 / ~할 의무가 있다
pretend to	~인 척하다	be willing to	기꺼이 ~하다
tend to	~하는 경향이 있다	be eager to	~하기를 열망하다
be about to	막 ~하려고 하다		

빈칸에 들어갈 영어 표현 또는 우리말 뜻을 적으시오.

표현	우리말 뜻	표현	우리말 뜻
happen to		be a_____ to	~할 수 있다
m_____ to	~을 해내다	be ready to	
seem to		be l_____ to	~하기 쉽다
f_____ to	~을 못하게 되다	be supposed to	
pretend to		be w_____ to	기꺼이 ~하다
t_____ to	~하는 경향이 있다	be eager to	
be about to			

β 다음 괄호 안에 단어들을 의미에 맞게 배열하시오.

① The runner (start / is / to / about).

_____

② He (like / seemed / to) the new song.

_____

③ She (know / to / pretended / not) them.

_____

④ We (fight / ready / are / to).

_____

⑤ She (him / to / meet / happened) in Italy.

_____

A 다음 빈칸에 알맞은 단어를 <보기>에서 찾아 쓰시오.

<보기>	eager / manage / pretended / supposed

① She _____ to be sick to skip the class.

② How many clothes did she _____ to wear?

③ The plane was _____ to arrive at noon, but it was delayed.

④ They were _____ to escape from the castle.

β 우리말 의미와 일치하도록 주어진 단어들을 올바르게 배열하시오.

① 그 버스가 막 출발하려고 한다.

(to / the / about / is / leave / bus)

_____

② 그 축구 선수는 기꺼이 가난한 사람들을 돕고자 했다.

(to / the / player / willing / help / was / soccer / poor / the)

_____

③ Jun은 거리에서 우연히 Jason을 만났다.

(Jun / Jason / to / the / street / meet / happened / on)

_____

A. 다음 빈칸을 예시처럼 채우시오.

표현	우리말 뜻	표현	우리말 뜻
happen to	우연히 ~하다	be able to	
manage to		be ready to	
seem to		be likely to	
fail to		be supposed to	
pretend to		be willing to	
tend to		be eager to	
be about to			

B. 다음 문장들을 우리말로 해석하시오.

① She pretended not to know them.

_____

② How many clothes did she manage to wear?

_____

③ The plane was supposed to arrive at noon, but it was delayed.

_____

④ The soccer player was willing to help the poor.

_____

정답 A의 정답은 앞 페이지의 오늘 공부했던 박스를 참고하세요. ① 그녀는 그들을 알지 못하는 척 했다. ② 그녀는 옷을 몇 벌이나 입는데 성공했나요? ③ 그 비행기는 정오에 도착하기로 되어있었지만, 연착되었다. ④ 그 축구 선수는 기꺼이 가난한 사람들을 돕고자 했다.

동명사 / to부정사를 좋아하는 동사

💡 혼공개념 동명사만을 목적어로 취하는 동사란?

1 뒤에 따라오는 목적어로 to부정사가 아닌 동명사(V-ing)를 선택하는 동사: enjoy, admit, mind, give up, finish, avoid, quit...

> 예 He enjoys playing board games. (to play)
> We didn't give up going up the hill. (to go)

💡 혼공개념 to부정사만을 목적어로 취하는 동사란?

1 뒤에 따라오는 목적어로 동명사가 아닌 to부정사를 선택하는 동사: hope, wish, want, expect, plan, decide, choose...

> 예 I expect to be busy tomorrow. (being)
> They wanted to see him more often. (seeing)

💡 혼공개념 동명사와 to부정사 모두를 목적어로 취하는 동사

1 뒤에 따라오는 목적어로 동명사와 to부정사가 모두 가능한 동사

> 1) 의미가 달라지지 않는 동사: 시작(begin, start), 좋고 싫음의 감정(like, love, hate)
>
> 예 It started to rain in the morning. (= raining)

> 2) 의미가 달라지는 동사

	+ 동명사	+ to부정사
forget, remember, regret	했던 일	할 일
try	(시험 삼아) 해보다	~하려고 노력하다
stop	~하는 것을 멈추다, 그만두다	~하기 위해 (하던 것을) 멈추다

> 예 I forgot locking the door.　　　　I forgot to lock the door.
> I tried sending her flowers.　　　I tried to send her flowers.
> He stopped talking to me.　　　　He stopped to talk to me.

다음 <보기> 속의 동사들을 제시된 조건에 맞게 분류하시오.

<보기>   try, stop, enjoy, choose, finish, quit, hope, wish, want, hate, forget, expect, plan, decide, begin, start, like, mind, give up, love, remember, avoid, regret

① 동명사만을 목적어로 취하는 동사

_____

② to부정사만을 목적어로 취하는 동사

_____

③ 동명사와 to부정사 모두를 목적어로 취하는 동사(의미 변화 없음)

_____

④ 동명사와 to부정사 모두를 목적어로 취하는 동사(의미 변화 있음)

_____

 다음 문장의 괄호 안에서 어법상 알맞은 표현을 선택하시오.

① He enjoys (playing / to play) board games.

② We didn't give up (going / to go) up the hill.

③ I expect (being / to be) busy tomorrow.

④ They wanted (seeing / to see) him more often.

⑤ It started (raining / to rain) in the morning.

⑥ I forgot (locking / to lock) the door.

⑦ I tried (sending / to send) her flowers.

⑧ He stopped (talking / to talk) to me.

(A) 빈칸에 괄호 안에 주어진 표현을 알맞게 변형하여 옮기시오.

① I finished _____.   (read the novel)

② My mom decided _____. (sell the car)

③ She loves _____. (play with those children)

(B) 다음 우리말과 일치하도록 괄호 안에 주어진 단어들 중 한 단어의 형태만 바꾼 다음 올바른 순서로 배열하시오.

① 나는 지난주에 Tom을 만났던 것을 기억할 수 없었다.

(meet / remember / week / Tom / I / last / couldn't)

_____

② 내 아버지는 마침내 담배를 끊으셨다.

(my / finally / smoke / gave / father / up)

_____

(C) 다음 사진을 보고 Kevin이 어머니에게 할 말을 완성하시오.

Kevin: Sorry, Mom.

I forgot _____.

(clean my room)

A. 다음 빈칸을 예시처럼 채우시오.

	+ 동명사	+ to부정사
forget, r_____, r_____	했던 일	
try		
stop		

B. 다음 문장의 괄호 안에서 어법상 알맞은 표현을 선택하시오.

① He enjoys (playing / to play) board games.

② We didn't give up (going / to go) up the hill.

③ I expect (being / to be) busy tomorrow.

④ They wanted (seeing / to see) him more often.

⑤ It started (raining / to rain) in the morning.

⑥ I forgot (locking / to lock) the door. (잠글 것을)

⑦ I tried (sending / to send) her flowers. (시험 삼아 보냄)

⑧ He stopped (talking / to talk) to me. (대화 중단)

⑨ I finished (reading / to read) the book.

⑩ My mom decided (selling / to sell) the car.

⑪ I couldn't remember (meeting / to meet) Tom last week.

정답 A의 정답은 앞 페이지의 오늘 공부했던 박스를 참고하세요. ① playing ② going ③ to be ④ to see ⑤ raining, to rain ⑥ to lock ⑦ sending ⑧ talking ⑨ reading ⑩ to sell ⑪ meeting

동명사 관용 구문

혼공개념 동명사의 관용적 구문이란?

1 사람들이 자주 쓰는 '동명사'가 들어가 있는 덩어리 표현

표현	우리말 뜻	표현	우리말 뜻
feel like ~ing	~하고 싶다	spend 시간/돈/노력 ~ing	~하는데 (시간/돈/노력)을 들이다
look forward to ~ing	~하는 것을 기대하다	be used to ~ing	~하는데 익숙하다
be busy ~ing	~하느라 바쁘다	cannot help ~ing	~하지 않을 수 없다

예 I feel like having Vietnamese noodles.

We looked forward to meeting you.

He is busy cleaning his room.

My parents spent all the money buying an apartment.

I'm used to getting up at six.

혼공 팁

'look forward to'와 'be used to'의 to는 전치사라서 반드시 그 뒤에 명사 또는 동명사가 와야 한다.

예 I'm looking forward to your future.

예외 The machine is used to examine patients.

2 cannot help ~ing 총정리

= cannot help(stop, avoid) ~ing = cannot but + 동사원형

= have no choice but to + 동사원형

예 I cannot help(stop, avoid) reading the next chapter.

= I cannot but read the next chapter.

= I have no choice but to read the next chapter.

빈칸에 알맞은 영어 단어를 쓰시오.

표현	우리말 뜻	표현	우리말 뜻
f_____ like ~ing	~하고 싶다	s_____ 시간/돈/노력 ~ing	~하는데 (시간/돈/노력)을 들이다
look f_____ to ~ing	~하는 것을 기대하다	be u_____ to ~ing	~하는데 익숙하다
be b_____ ~ing	~하느라 바쁘다	cannot h_____ ~ing	~하지 않을 수 없다

β 다음 문장에서 어법상 <u>잘못된</u> 한 단어를 찾아 밑줄을 긋고 바르게 고치시오.

① I feel like have Vietnamese noodles.

_____

② We looked forward to meet you.

_____

③ He is busy clean his room.

_____

④ My parents spent all the money buy an apartment.

_____

⑤ I'm used to get up at six.

_____

⑥ I cannot help read the next chapter.

_____

다음 괄호 안에서 알맞은 것을 고르시오.

① The boys are looking forward to (meet / meeting) her.

② We are not used to (eat / eating) spicy food.

③ The kids were not used to (listen / listening) to your scary stories.

④ The money will be used to (help / helping) the poor.

⑤ She couldn't help (tell / telling) the truth to her family.

β 다음 우리말과 일치하도록 괄호 안에 주어진 단어들 중 한 단어의 형태만 바꾼 다음 올바른 순서로 배열하시오.

① 그녀는 울고 싶었다.

(cry / felt / like / she)

_____

② 엄마는 부엌에서 요리하시느라 바빴다.

(kitchen / was / cook / the / mom / busy / in)

_____

③ 그 경찰은 그가 무엇을 하고 있는 중이었는지 궁금한 생각을 떨칠 수 없었다.

(he / the / officer / couldn't / police / was / help / doing / wonder / what)

_____

A. 다음 빈칸을 예시처럼 채우시오.

표현	우리말 뜻	표현	우리말 뜻
feel like ~ing	~하고 싶다	s_____ 시간/돈/노력 ~ing	~하는데 (시간/돈/노력)을 들이다
look f_____ to ~ing	~하는 것을 기대하다	be u_____ to ~ing	~하는데 익숙하다
be b_____ ~ing		cannot help ~ing	

B. 다음 문장에서 어법상 잘못된 한 단어를 찾아 밑줄을 긋고 바르게 고치시오.

① We looked forward to meet you.

_____

② I'm used to get up at six.

_____

③ I cannot help read the next chapter.

_____

④ We are not used to eat spicy food.

_____

⑤ The money will be used to helping the poor.

_____

⑥ Mom was busy cook in the kitchen.

_____

정답 A의 정답은 앞 페이지의 오늘 공부했던 박스를 참고하세요. ① meet → meeting ② get → getting ③ read → reading ④ eat → eating
⑤ helping → help ⑥ cook → cooking

현재분사 / 과거분사

 현재분사란?

1 현재분사: 동사 + ing의 형태로 아래와 같이 쓰임

   1) 진행형: 주로 be동사 + ~ing

     예 He was riding a bike.

  2) 명사 수식: 명사의 앞이나 뒤에서 '~하는, ~하고 있는'으로 쓰임

     예 There is a sleeping puppy. (puppy 수식)

      Can you see the boy sleeping on the couch? (the boy 수식)

혼공개념 과거분사란?

1 과거분사: 주로 동사의 과거분사(p.p.) 형태로 쓰임

   1) 완료: 동작이 이미 끝난 경우

     예 He collected some fallen leaves.

      This is a broken mirror.

  2) 수동: 동작의 영향을 받거나, 당할 때 쓰임

     예 My wallet was stolen.

혼공 팁

우리말과 달리 영어에서는 뒤에서 수식하는 경우가 많다. 주로 '현재/과거분사 + 전치사구
(시간, 장소, 기타)'로 수식하는 말이 길어질 때 뒤에서 수식한다.

  예 Can you see the boy sleeping on the couch?

    Finally, I opened the door locked from inside.

혼공 연습

A 다음 우리말과 일치하도록 빈칸에 주어진 단어를 알맞은 형태로 바꾸어 쓰시오.

① 잠자고 있는 강아지   a _____ dog (sleep)

② 낙엽(떨어진 잎들)   _____ leaves (fall)

③ 깨진 거울   a _____ mirror (break)

④ 잠긴 문   a _____ door (lock)

B 다음 괄호 안에 주어진 말의 알맞은 형태를 쓰시오.

① He was looking at the (run) water.

_____

② He decided to buy a (use) car.

_____

③ She hates a (bark) dog.

_____

C 다음 빈칸에 알맞은 말을 <보기>에서 골라 형태를 변형하여 쓰시오.

<보기>	stand paint play

① The picture _____ by Jessy will be sold.

② Who is the boy _____ baseball over there?

③ Don't talk with the man _____ behind the tree.

A 다음 문장에서 어법상 <u>잘못된</u> 한 단어를 찾아 밑줄을 긋고 바르게 고치시오.

① The pirates found a lot of hiding treasure.

_____

② What is the language speaking in Vietnam?

_____

③ The police are looking for the escape prisoners.

_____

β 우리말 의미와 일치하도록 주어진 단어들을 올바르게 배열하시오.

① Jessy의 의해 그려진 그림은 판매될 것이다.

(will / by / Jessy / painted / be / sold)
The picture _____.

② 저기에서 야구를 하고 있는 소년은 누구니?

(playing / is / the / there / boy / over / baseball)
Who _____?

③ 나무 뒤에 서 있는 그 남자와 말하지 마라.

(with / behind / talk / standing / tree / man / the / the)
Don't _____.

④ 그는 낙엽을 쓸어 모았다.

(the / collected / leaves / he / fallen)

_____.

⑤ 바이올린을 연주하고 있는 소녀는 내 여동생이다.

(the / violin / the / girl / playing / sister / is / my)

_____.

A. 다음 문장의 괄호 안에서 어법상 알맞은 표현을 선택하시오.

① He was (riding / ridden) a bike.

② There is a (sleeping / slept) puppy.

③ This is a (breaking / broken) mirror.

④ Finally, I opened the door (locking / locked) from inside.

B. 다음 문장들을 우리말로 해석하시오.

⑤ He decided to buy a used car.

_____

⑥ The picture painted by Jessy will be sold.

_____

⑦ Who is the boy playing baseball over there?

_____

⑧ Don't talk with the man standing behind the tree.

_____

⑨ The police are looking for the escaped prisoners.

_____

정답 ① riding ② sleeping ③ broken ④ locked ⑤ 그는 중고차를 사기로 결정했다. ⑥ Jessy의 의해 그려진 그림은 판매될 것이다. ⑦ 저기
에서 야구를 하고 있는 소년은 누구니? ⑧ 나무 뒤에 서 있는 그 남자와 말하지 마라. ⑨ 경찰들은 탈옥한 죄수들을 찾고 있는 중이다.

분사구문 1

혼공개념 분사구문이란?

1 원리: 분사(~ing / p.p.)를 사용해서 문장을 간단하게 줄여 표현하는 방식

예 ~~While he~~ walked home, Jun bought some bananas.

= Walking home, Jun bought some bananas.

혼공개념 분사구문의 해석

1 분사구문을 만들면서 생략된 접속사의 의미를 살려 해석함

1) 시간: when, while, as ...

예 When she saw me on the street, she started to cry.

= Seeing me on the street, she started to cry.

2) 이유: since, as, because

예 As I was tired, I woke up late in the morning.

= Being tired, I woke up late in the morning.

3) 조건: if

예 If you turn to the left, you will find an ATM machine.

= Turning to the left, you will find an ATM machine.

4) 양보: though, although(실제로 많이 쓰이지 않음)

예 Though she was sick, Kelly had to work.

= Being sick, Kelly had to work.

혼공 팁

분사구문을 만들 때 Being, Having been은 생략 가능하다.

예 Being tired, I woke up late in the morning.

= Tired, I woke up late in the morning.

Part 1

혼공 연습

A 다음 밑줄 친 부분을 분사구문으로 다시 쓰시오.

① <u>While he walked home</u>, Jun bought some bananas.

_____

② <u>When she saw me on the street</u>, she started to cry.

_____

③ <u>As I was tired</u>, I woke up late in the morning.

_____

B 밑줄 친 분사구문과 같은 의미를 가지도록 빈칸을 완성하시오.

① <u>Turning to the left</u>, you will find an ATM machine.

If _____

② <u>Being sick</u>, Kelly had to work.

_____

C 괄호 안의 단어들을 알맞게 배열하여 분사구문을 완성하시오.

① (the / at / hotel / arriving), she met her client.

_____

② (listening / music / to), he washed the dishes.

_____

A 다음 두 문장이 같은 뜻이 되도록, 괄호 안에서 알맞은 단어를 고르시오.

① Catching a cold, Jun couldn't go to school.

= (As / Though) he caught a cold, Jun couldn't go to school.

② Feeling happy, Melanie plays the piano.

= (When / Though) she feels happy, Melanie plays the piano.

B 다음 밑줄 친 부분에서 어법상 잘못된 부분을 찾아 바르게 고치시오.

① <u>Open the door</u>, I found a sleeping cat on the couch.

_____

② <u>Get up late</u>, she missed the first train.

_____

C 의미가 같도록 주어진 단어를 알맞게 빈칸에 배열하시오.

① Being thirsty, the boy drank a glass of water.

= _____, the boy drank a glass of water.

(he / thirsty / since / was)

② Raised in England, he speaks English.

= _____, he speaks English.

(raised / he / England / because / was / in)

A. 밑줄 친 분사구문의 용법을 '시간, 이유, 조건, 양보' 중 하나 골라 적으시오.

① <u>Walking home</u>, Jun bought some bananas.　　＿＿＿＿＿

② <u>Seeing me on the road</u>, he started to cry.　　＿＿＿＿＿

③ <u>Being tired</u>, I woke up late in the morning.　　＿＿＿＿＿

④ <u>Turning to the left</u>, you will find an ATM machine.　　＿＿＿＿＿

⑤ <u>Being sick</u>, Kelly had to work.　　＿＿＿＿＿

B. 다음 문장들을 우리말로 해석하시오.

⑥ Arriving at the hotel, she met her client.

＿＿＿＿＿＿＿＿＿＿＿＿＿＿＿＿＿＿＿＿＿＿＿＿＿＿

⑦ Catching a cold, Jun couldn't go to school.

＿＿＿＿＿＿＿＿＿＿＿＿＿＿＿＿＿＿＿＿＿＿＿＿＿＿

⑧ Raised in England, he speaks English.

＿＿＿＿＿＿＿＿＿＿＿＿＿＿＿＿＿＿＿＿＿＿＿＿＿＿

정답　① 시간　② 시간　③ 이유　④ 조건　⑤ 양보　⑥ 호텔에 도착했을 때, 그녀는 그녀의 고객을 만났다.　⑦ 감기에 걸렸기 때문에, Jun은 학교에 갈 수 없었다.　⑧ 영국에서 자랐기 때문에, 그는 영어로 말한다.

분사구문 2

혼공개념 분사구문의 부정

1 방법: 분사(~ing/p.p.) 앞에 not 또는 never을 써서 부정함

 As he didn't know her name, he couldn't talk to her.

⇒ Not knowing her name, he couldn't talk to her.

혼공개념 주어가 다른 분사구문

1 부사절의 주어와 주절의 주어가 다르면 분사구에 다른 주어를 표현함

 If the weather is good, we can climb the mountain.

⇒ The weather being good, we can climb the mountain.

As the store was closed, we had to stay home all day.

⇒ The store being closed, we had to stay home all day.

혼공개념 시제가 다른 완료형 분사구문

1 부사절이 주절보다 시제가 앞서면 Having + p.p.를 씀

 Since he studied English in Canada, he speaks English fluently.
　　　　　　　　　1　　　　　　　　　　　　　　　　2

⇒ Having studied English in Canada, he speaks English fluently.

훈공 연습

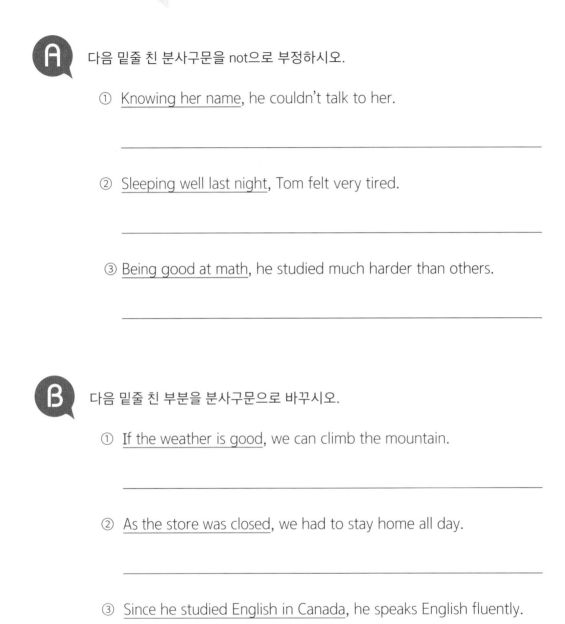

A 다음 밑줄 친 분사구문을 not으로 부정하시오.

① <u>Knowing her name</u>, he couldn't talk to her.

_____

② <u>Sleeping well last night</u>, Tom felt very tired.

_____

③ <u>Being good at math</u>, he studied much harder than others.

_____

β 다음 밑줄 친 부분을 분사구문으로 바꾸시오.

① <u>If the weather is good</u>, we can climb the mountain.

_____

② <u>As the store was closed</u>, we had to stay home all day.

_____

③ <u>Since he studied English in Canada</u>, he speaks English fluently.

_____

A 다음 밑줄 친 부분을 분사구문으로 바꾸시오.

① Since it was cold, we went back home early.

_____

② Though he was young, he was smart enough to understand it.

_____

③ If the weather is fine, let's go out and play.

_____

B 의미가 같도록 주어진 단어를 알맞게 빈칸에 배열하시오.

① As I haven't saved enough money, I can't buy the car.

= _____, I can't buy the car.

(saved / enough / having / not / money)

② After I had finished reading the report, I took a shower.

= _____, I took a shower.

(reading / having / report / finished / the)

③ Since he was raised in China, he knows how to use chopsticks.

= _____, he knows how to use chopsticks.

(raised / China / been / in / having)

A. 다음 밑줄 친 부분을 분사구문으로 바꾸시오.

① Since he didn't sleep well last night, Tom felt very tired.

_____

② If the weather is good, we can climb the mountain.

_____

③ Since he was raised in China, he knows how to use chopsticks.

_____

B. 다음 문장들을 우리말로 해석하시오.

④ Having studied English in Canada, he speaks English fluently.

_____

⑤ Not being good at math, he studied much harder than others.

_____

⑥ Being young, he was smart enough to understand it.

_____

⑦ Having finished reading the report, I took a shower.

_____

정답 ① Not sleeping well last night ② The weather being good ③ Having been raised in China ④ 캐나다에서 영어를 공부했기 때문에 그는 영어를 유창하게 말한다. ⑤ 수학을 잘하지 못했기 때문에, 그는 남들보다 더 열심히 공부했다. ⑥ 어렸음에도 불구하고, 그는 그것을 이해할 만큼 충분히 똑똑했다. ⑦ 그 보고서 읽기를 끝내고 나서, 나는 샤워를 했다.

관계대명사 심화 1

 혼공개념 주격 관계대명사란?

1 주격 관계대명사: 관계절을 이끌며, 그 속에서 주어 역할을 함

예 This is <u>my brother</u> who(that) ▲ is a doctor.
　　　　선행사

　　That is <u>the magic house</u> which(that) ▲ has a lot of wooden doors.
　　　　　　　선행사

 혼공개념 목적격 관계대명사란?

1 목적격 관계대명사: 관계절을 이끌며, 그 속에서 동사나 전치사의 목적어 역할을 함

예 <u>The pillow</u> which(that) he is holding ▲ is mine.
　　선행사

　　Do you know <u>the boy</u> whom(that) Jun is talking with ▲ ?
　　　　　　　　선행사

 혼공개념 소유격 관계사란?

1 소유격 관계사: 관계절 안에서 뒤에 나온 명사를 수식하며, 그 명사와 선행사의 소유 관계를 나타냄

예 I met <u>a girl</u> whose dream is to be a traveller.
　　　선행사

　　<u>The building</u> whose design I love is amazing.
　　선행사

	사람	동물, 사물	사람, 동물, 사물
주격	who	which	that
목적격	who(m)	which	that
소유격	whose	whose / of which	-

괄호 안에서 알맞은 관계사를 고르시오.

① That is the magic house (who / which / whose) has a lot of wooden doors.

② This is my brother (who / which / whose) is a doctor.

③ The pillow (who / which / whose) he is holding is mine.

④ Do you know the boy (which / that / whose) Jun is talking with?

 적절한 관계사를 사용하여 두 문장을 합치시오.

① I met a girl. + Her dream is to be a traveller.

_____

② The building is amazing. + I love its design.

_____

③ Tom was a businessman. + His mom was a teacher.

_____

④ I know a boy. + His brother is a singer.

_____

C 다음 표의 빈칸에 들어갈 알맞은 관계사를 쓰시오.

	사람	동물, 사물	사람, 동물, 사물
주격			that
목적격	who(m)		
소유격		whose / of which	-

A 다음 괄호 안에 주어진 말들을 올바른 순서로 배열하시오.

① This is my brother _____.

(a / who / doctor / is)

② The mother _____ tried to hug him.

(crying / whose / was / son)

③ English is a language _____.

(to / I / found / difficult / that / learn)

B 다음 우리말과 일치하도록 영작하시오.

① 전화로 통화하고 있는 남자를 봐라.

Look at the man _____.

② 이것은 내가 어제 샀던 그 잡지이다. (bought)

This is the magazine _____.

③ 이름이 Nancy인 젊은 숙녀가 내일 우리를 방문할 것이다.

A young lady _____ will visit us tomorrow.

C 다음 문장에서 어법상 틀린 단어를 찾아 밑줄을 긋고 바르게 고치시오.

① English is a language whose Jun wants to learn.

_____

② They are people which study hard to pass the test.

_____

A. 다음 빈칸을 예시처럼 채우시오.

	사람	동물, 사물	사람, 동물, 사물
주격	who		
목적격			
소유격			

B. 빈칸에 알맞은 관계사를 쓰시오.

① The pillow _____ he is holding is mine.

② The mother _____ son was crying tried to hug him.

C. 다음 문장들을 우리말로 해석하시오.

③ Do you know the boy that Jun is talking with?

_____

④ I met a girl whose dream is to be a traveller.

_____

⑤ English is a language that I found difficult to learn.

_____

⑥ This is the magazine that I bought yesterday.

_____

⑦ A young lady whose name is Nancy will visit us tomorrow.

_____

정답 A의 정답은 앞 페이지의 오늘 공부했던 박스를 참고하세요. ① which(that) ② whose ③ 너는 Jun이 함께 이야기 나누고 있는 그 소년을 아니? ④ 나는 꿈이 여행가인 한 소녀를 만났다. ⑤ 영어는 내가 배우기 어렵다고 여겼던 언어이다. ⑥ 이것은 내가 어제 샀던 그 잡지이다. ⑦ 이름이 Nancy인 젊은 숙녀가 내일 우리를 방문할 것이다.

관계대명사 심화 2

관계대명사 that만 사용하는 경우란?

1 선행사의 특성에 따라 관계대명사 that만을 사용하는 경우를 말함

1) 선행사가 사람+동물, 사람+사물인 경우

Look at the <u>boy and his dog</u> that are walking to us.

2) 선행사에 서수가 있는 경우

He is <u>the first man</u> that landed on the Moon.

3) 선행사에 최상급이 있는 경우

This is the <u>most beautiful music</u> that I've ever listened to.

4) 선행사에 all, any, the very, the only, the same, no 등이 있을 때

He spent <u>all the money</u> that he earned.

관계대명사 what이란?

1 선행사를 포함한 관계대명사로 the thing which(that)으로 표현할 수 있고, '~ 것'으로 해석함

예 He showed me <u>what</u> was in his pocket.

=> He showed me <u>the thing which(that)</u> was in his pocket.

He gave her <u>what</u> she needed.

=> He gave her <u>the thing which(that)</u> she needed.

혼공 연습

 다음 괄호 안에서 어법상 알맞은 단어를 고르고 우리말로 해석하시오.

① This is the most beautiful music (what / that) I've ever listened to.

_____

② He gave her (what / that) she needed.

_____

③ He spent all the money (what / that) he earned.

_____

④ Look at the boy and his dog (what / that) are walking to us.

_____

⑤ He is the only student (what / that) can speak Russian in our class.

_____

⑥ Did you understand (what / that) he said?

_____

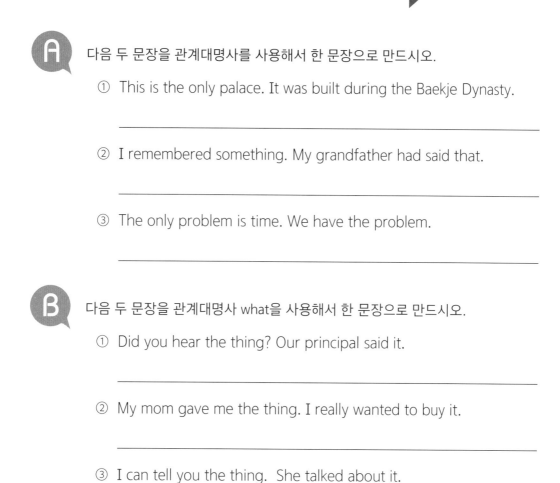

A 다음 두 문장을 관계대명사를 사용해서 한 문장으로 만드시오.

① This is the only palace. It was built during the Baekje Dynasty.

_____

② I remembered something. My grandfather had said that.

_____

③ The only problem is time. We have the problem.

_____

B 다음 두 문장을 관계대명사 what을 사용해서 한 문장으로 만드시오.

① Did you hear the thing? Our principal said it.

_____

② My mom gave me the thing. I really wanted to buy it.

_____

③ I can tell you the thing. She talked about it.

_____

C 우리말 의미와 일치하도록 주어진 단어들을 올바르게 배열하시오.

① Tom이 그녀에게 하길 원하는 것은 가능한 일이다.

(her / Tom / do / wants / what / to) is possible.

_____

② 나를 흥미롭게 했던 것은 그의 태도였다.

(me / what / interested) was his behavior.

_____

A. 빈칸에 알맞은 관계사를 선택하시오.

① This is the most beautiful music (what / that) I've ever listened to.

② He gave her (what / that) she needed.

③ He spent all the money (what / that) he earned.

④ He is the only student (what / that) can speak Russian in our class.

B. 다음 문장들을 우리말로 해석하시오.

⑤ The only problem that we have is time.

_____

⑥ This is the only palace that was built during the Baekje Dynasty.

_____

⑦ My mom gave me what I really wanted to buy.

_____

⑧ What interested me was his behavior.

_____

정답 ① that ② what ③ that ④ that ⑤ 우리가 가지고 있는 유일한 문제는 시간이다. ⑥ 이것은 백제 왕조에 지어졌던 유일한 궁궐이다.
⑦ 우리 엄마는 내가 정말 사고 싶어했던 것을 나에게 주었다. ⑧ 나를 흥미롭게 했던 것은 그의 태도였다.

관계부사

 관계대명사 VS 관계부사

1 관계대명사: 두 문장을 같은 의미의 명사를 활용하여 한 문장으로 합칠 때 사용함

예 That is <u>the magic house</u> which(that) has a lot of wooden doors.
   　　　　　　선행사　　　　　관계대명사

2 관계부사: '전치사 + 관계대명사'를 한 단어로 줄여서 나타낸 것으로 역시 두 문장을 한 문장으로 합칠 때 사용함

예 This is the building. John works in the building(there).

   = This is <u>the building</u> where(in which) John works.
   　　　　　　선행사　　　　　　관계부사

 관계부사의 종류

선행사	관계부사
장소(place)	where
시간(time)	when
이유(reason)	why
방법(way)	how

예 January is <u>the month</u>. It is really cold in January(then).

   = January is the month when it is really cold.

   That is <u>the reason</u>. He is always late for the reason.

   = That is the reason why he is always late.

   This is <u>the way</u>. He fixes a computer easily in that way.

   = This is the way (how) he fixes a computer easily.

혼공 팁

관계부사 how와 선행사 the way는 보통 같이 쓰지 않는다. 그래서 the way만 쓰거나 how 만 쓰니 기억해 두자.

다음 <보기>처럼 관계부사를 사용해서 두 문장을 결합하시오.

> <보기>　　　This is the building. + John works there.
>
> ⇒ This is the building where John works.

① January is the month. + It is really cold in January.

_____

② That is the reason. + He is always late for the reason.

_____

③ New York is the city. + I lived there when I was seven years old.

_____

④ This is the store. + I bought the shampoo there.

_____

⑤ Gimhae is the city. + I was born there.

_____

⑥ This is the way. + He fixes a computer easily in that way.

_____

다음 괄호 안에서 알맞은 것을 고르시오.

① Spring is the best season (which / when) we can go hiking.

② October is the month (which / when) comes after September.

③ I visited the house (which / where) Mozart was born.

④ I like the doctors (that / why) took care of my mom.

 다음 표현들을 의미가 가장 자연스럽게 이어지도록 선으로 연결하시오.

① Tell me the reason   ⓐ when the weather was good.

② The morning is the time   ⓑ why you left me.

③ I visited London in July   ⓒ when I like to read books most.

C 다음 괄호 안의 단어들을 알맞게 배열하시오.

① This is (born / Jun / where / was).

_____

② That is (regularly / why / to / we / work / have / out).

_____

③ Do you remember the restaurant (met / you / John / where)?

_____

혼공
복습

A. 다음 빈칸을 예시처럼 채우시오.

선행사	관계부사
장소(place)	where
시간(time)	
이유(reason)	
방법(way)	

B. 빈칸에 알맞은 관계사를 선택하시오.

① October is the month (which / when) comes after September.

② I like the doctors (that / why) took care of my mom.

③ Tell me the reason (which / why) you left me.

C. 관계부사를 사용해서 두 문장을 결합하시오.

④ January is the month. + It is really cold in January.

_____

⑤ This is the store. + I bought the shampoo there.

_____

⑥ New York is the city. + I lived there when I was 7.

_____

정답 A의 정답은 앞 페이지의 오늘 공부했던 박스를 참고하세요. ① which ② that ③ why ④ January is the month when it is really cold.
⑤ This is the store where I bought the shampoo. ⑥ New York is the city where I lived when I was 7.

관계사의 한정적(제한적) / 계속적 용법

> 🔍 **혼공개념** 관계사의 한정적(제한적) 용법이란?

1 한정적(제한적)용법: 선행사를 수식하는 역할을 함

1) 관계대명사의 한정적(제한적) 용법

예 I met a professor. He wanted to work with me.

= I met a professor who wanted to work with me.

2) 관계부사의 한정적(제한적) 용법

예 This is the city. He was born in the city.

= This is the city where he was born.

> 🔍 **혼공개념** 관계사의 계속적 용법이란?

1 계속적 용법: 콤마(,) 다음에 관계사가 쓰이는 경우이며, 선행사에 대해 추가 정보를 제공함

1) 관계대명사의 계속적 용법

예 This book was written by Jun, who lived a happy life.

2) 관계부사의 계속적 용법

예 She went to Seattle, where she studied architecture.

혼공 팁

관계대명사의 한정적 용법과 계속적 용법은 아래 예문으로 그 차이를 이해할 수 있다.

예) He has two daughters who became doctors.(한정적 용법)

He has two daughters, who became doctors.(계속적 용법)

Part 1

혼공 연습

 다음 밑줄 친 부분을 알맞은 관계부사로 고쳐 쓰시오.

① This is the city <u>in which</u> he was born.

② We will visit the Hanok Village, <u>in which</u> we had fun.

③ This is the Italian restaurant, <u>in which</u> they serve really good spaghetti.

④ Tell me the reason <u>for which</u> you didn't show up.

⑤ This is my uncle's farm <u>on which</u> you can see a lot of animals.

β 다음 두 문장이 같은 뜻이 되도록 빈칸에 알맞은 말을 쓰시오.

① This book was written by Jun and he lived a happy life.

= This book was written by Jun, _____.

② She went to Seattle _____.

= She went to Seattle, where she studied architecture.

③ He has two daughters _____.

= He has two daughters, who became doctors.

A 다음 밑줄 친 부분을 알맞은 관계부사로 고쳐 쓰시오.

① This is the house in which Lincoln grew up.

_____

② I still remember the time at which I met you in the park.

_____

B 빈칸에 알맞은 관계사를 쓰시오.

① They played soccer last Sunday, _____ it rained a lot.

② Jun graduated in 2017, _____ jobs were hard to find.

③ Chloe went to Toronto, _____ she studied English.

C 다음 우리말과 일치하도록 괄호 안의 말을 알맞게 배열하시오.

① 포항에 지진이 있었는데, 그것은 나쁜 소식이었다.
There was an earthquake in Pohang, _____.
(news / which / bad / was)

② 당신은 장마 기간 동안 반드시 충분한 물을 저장해야 하는데, 그 기간은 대략 2달 정도 지속된다.
You must store enough water during the rainy season,

_____.

(lasts / which / months / about / two)

A. 다음 밑줄 친 부분을 알맞은 관계부사로 고쳐 쓰시오.

① We will visit the Hanok Village, <u>in which</u> we had fun.

_____

② This is the Italian restaurant, <u>in which</u> they serve really good spaghetti.

_____

③ Tell me the reason <u>for which</u> you didn't show up.

_____

④ This is my uncle's farm <u>on which</u> you can see a lot of animals.

_____

B. 다음 문장들을 우리말로 해석하시오.

⑤ He has two daughters, who became doctors.

_____

⑥ I still remember the time when I met you in the park.

_____

⑦ Jun graduated in 2017, when jobs were hard to find.

_____

⑧ You must store enough water during the rainy season, which lasts
  about two months.

_____

상관접속사

🔍 혼공개념 상관접속사란?

1 상관접속사: 두 개의 단어 A, B를 짝지어서 표현할 수 있도록 쓰는 접속사

> 예 He is <u>not only</u> brave <u>but also</u> intelligent. (0)
>   A   B

혼공 팁

상관접속사를 쓸 때 A와 B는 같은 형태가 되어야 한다.

He is <u>not only</u> brave <u>but also</u> intelligence. (X)
           A   B

🔍 혼공개념 상관접속사의 종류

표현	의미	동사의 수 일치
both A and B	A, B 둘 다	복수동사
either A or B	A 또는 B	B에 일치
neither A nor B	A, B 둘 다 아닌	B에 일치
not A but B	A가 아니라 B	B에 일치
not only A but (also) B	A뿐만 아니라 B도	B에 일치
B as well as A		

1 Both Tom and Judy <u>like</u> playing board games.
        A   B

2 Either she or I <u>have</u> to decide what to buy for the trip.
           A   B

3 Neither Jake nor I <u>was</u> interested in that show.
            A   B

4 Not you but he <u>is</u> going to perform.
        A   B

5 Not only Chloe but (also) her students <u>were</u> happy with the result.
            A   B

다음 표의 빈칸을 채우시오.

표현	의미
both A and B	
either A or B	
neither A nor B	
not A but B	
not only A but (also) B	
B as well as A	

β 다음 괄호 속에서 어법상 알맞은 단어를 고르시오.

① Both Tom and Judy (like / likes) playing board games.

② Either she or I (have / has) to decide what to buy for the trip.

③ Neither Jake nor I (was / are) interested in that show.

④ Not you but he (is / are) going to perform.

⑤ Not only Chloe but her students (was / were) happy with the result.

⑥ Neither Coke nor Sprite (is / are) harmful for your health.

⑦ He is not only brave but also (intelligent / intelligence).

A 다음 빈칸에 알맞은 말을 <보기>에서 찾아 쓰시오.

<보기>	but / both / neither / either

① _____ John and Jane are doing well at school.

② _____ you or she has to walk the dog.

③ Jun is not handsome _____ cute.

④ _____ Jake nor I liked P.E.

B 다음 우리말과 일치하도록 괄호 안에 주어진 말들을 올바른 순서로 배열하시오.

① 이번에는 네가 아니라 그가 노래를 해야 한다.

(but / you / has / not / he)

_____ to sing this time.

② 너희들은 지금 먹거나 콘서트가 끝난 후에 먹어야 한다.

You guys should either _____.

(eat / eat / or / concert / after / now / the)

③ 연필들뿐만 아니라 지우개도 그들을 위해 제공되어진다.

_____ provided for them.

(are / erasers / pencils / as well as)

C 다음 괄호 속에서 어법상 알맞은 것을 고르시오.

① Either you or Kevin (has / have) to wash the dishes.

② The students as well as the teacher (was / were) satisfied with it.

③ Both soccer and basketball (is / are) my favorite sports.

혼공
복습

A. 다음 빈칸을 예시처럼 채우시오.

표현	의미	동사의 수 일치
both A and B	A, B 둘 다	복수동사
either A or B		
neither A nor B		
not A but B		
not only A but (also) B		
B as well as A		

B. 다음 문장들을 우리말로 해석하시오.

① Either she or I have to decide what to buy for the trip.

_____

② Not only Chloe but her students were happy with the result.

_____

③ Neither Coke nor Sprite is harmful for your health.

_____

④ Either you or she has to walk the dog.

_____

⑤ You guys should either eat now or eat after the concert.

_____

⑥ Erasers as well as pencils are provided for them.

_____

정답 A의 정답은 앞 페이지의 오늘 공부했던 박스를 참고하세요. ① 그녀 또는 내가 그 여행을 위해 무엇을 살지 결정해야 한다. ② Chloe뿐만 아니라 그녀의 학생들도 그 결과에 행복했다. ③ 콜라와 스프라이트 둘 다 당신의 건강에 해롭지않다. ④ 너 또는 그녀가 강아지를 산책시켜야 한다. ⑤ 너희들은 지금 먹거나 콘서트가 끝난 후에 먹어야 한다. ⑥ 연필들뿐만 아니라 지우개도 그들을 위해 제공되어진다.

현재완료 / 과거완료

혼공개념 현재완료란?

1 현재완료: 과거의 행동이 현재와 연관이 있는 것을 표현할 때 have(has) + p.p.로 씀

예 I have already finished my homework.

I have learned English since I was 10 years old.

혼공개념 과거완료란?

1 과거에 일어난 일보다 더 앞서 일어난 일(대과거)이 과거와 연관이 있는 것을 표현할 때 had + p.p.로 씀

예 When I came back, she had already gone out.

She had never been to Canada until then.

I hadn't seen him for a long time.

I didn't know that he had lost his key.

2 과거보다 더 앞선 일(대과거)을 분명히 표현하고 싶을 때 자주 씀

예 She had already finished the work when I arrived.

　　　먼저 일어남　　　　　　　　　　나중에 일어남

혼공 연습

A 다음 <보기> 안의 동사를 참고하여 빈칸에 의미상 적절한 과거완료를 쓰시오.

<보기>	go see lose be

① When I came back, she _____ already _____ out.

② She _____ never _____ to Canada until then.

③ I _____ not _____ him for a long time.

④ I didn't know that he _____ _____ his key.

B 다음 밑줄 친 사건 중 먼저 일어난 것에 1, 나중에 일어난 것에 2라고 쓰시오.

① When <u>I came back</u>, <u>she had already gone out</u>.
     (　)   (　)

② <u>I didn't know</u> that <u>he had lost his key</u>.
     (　)   (　)

③ <u>She had already finished the work</u> when <u>I arrived</u>.
        (　)   (　)

④ <u>The concert had already begun</u> when <u>they got to the stadium</u>.
         (　)   (　)

A 다음 밑줄 친 부분을 어법상 바르게 고치시오.

① When I got to the bus stop, <u>the bus has already left</u>.

_____

② I knew who the man was. <u>I has had lunch with him once</u>.

_____

③ The classroom was pretty dirty. <u>It was not cleaned</u> for a week.

_____

B 다음 우리말에 맞게 주어진 단어를 사용하여 빈칸을 채우시오.

① 내가 전화했을 때 그녀는 이미 그 알약을 먹은 상태였다.

When I called her, she _____ the pill. (take)

② 내가 공항에 도착했을 때, 그 비행기는 이미 떠나버렸었다.

When I got to the airport, the plane _____. (leave)

C 다음 사진을 보고 빈칸을 알맞은 단어로 채우시오.

He gave _____ all the _____ that
he _____ _____. (save)

A. 다음 동사를 <보기>처럼 과거완료 시제로 바꾸어 쓰시오.

① eat	had eaten	⑥ finish	
② save		⑦ have	
③ be		⑧ leave	
④ lose		⑨ begin	
⑤ see		⑩ take	

B. 다음 밑줄 친 사건 중 먼저 일어난 것에 1, 나중에 일어난 것에 2라고 쓰시오.

⑪ <u>I didn't know</u> that <u>he had lost his key</u>.
    ( )   ( )

⑫ <u>The concert had already begun</u> when <u>they got to the stadium</u>.
        ( )   ( )

C. 다음 밑줄 친 부분을 어법상 바르게 고치시오.

⑬ I knew who the man was. I <u>has had</u> lunch with him once.
_____

⑭ The classroom was pretty dirty. It <u>was not cleaned</u> for a week.
_____

수일치

> 💡 **혼공개념** 단수 취급하는 경우

1 다음과 같은 경우 주어를 단수 취급함

　　1) every, each + 단수명사　　　　Each answer **is** worth 10 points.

　　2) 과목명, 국가 이름, 책이름　　　Physics **is** one of my favorite subjects.

　　3) 시간, 거리, 무게, 가격　　　　Fifty dollars **is** better than nothing.

　　4) 두 개의 명사로 이루어진 하나의 개념　　Bread and butter **is** good for breakfast.

　　5) 주어의 역할을 하는 명사구(동명사, to부정사)　　Playing baseball **is** exciting.

> 💡 **혼공개념** 복수 취급하는 경우

1 a number of 복수명사

　　There **are** a number of people on the street.

2 the 형용사 = 복수명사

　　The rich **are** not always happy.

　　혼공 팁

　　the number of + '명사'는 '~의 숫자'를 의미하기 때문에 단수 취급해야 한다.

　　[예] The number of people **has** increased.

> 💡 **혼공개념** of 이하의 명사의 수에 주목하는 경우

1 <u>some of, a lot of, all of, most of, half of</u> + 단수 / 복수명사

　　[예] Half of the apple **was** rotten.

　　　　Half of the apples **were** rotten.

다음 괄호 안에서 어법상 알맞은 단어를 고르시오.

① Each answer (is / are) worth 10 points.

② Physics (is / are) one of my favorite subjects.

③ Fifty dollars (is / are) better than nothing.

④ Bread and butter (is / are) good for breakfast.

⑤ There (is / are) a number of people on the street.

⑥ Linguistics (is / are) a study of languages.

⑦ *Romeo and Juliet* (is / are) a sad story.

⑧ Two miles (is / are) a long distance to walk.

B 다음 밑줄 친 단어를 어법상 알맞게 고치시오.

① The rich <u>is</u> not always happy.　　　　＿＿＿＿＿＿＿＿

② Half of the buildings <u>was</u> destroyed.　　　＿＿＿＿＿＿＿＿

③ The number of people <u>have</u> increased.　　　＿＿＿＿＿＿＿＿

④ Half of the apple <u>were</u> rotten.　　　　＿＿＿＿＿＿＿＿

⑤ Half of the apples <u>was</u> rotten.　　　　＿＿＿＿＿＿＿＿

A 다음 괄호 안에서 어법상 알맞은 단어를 고르시오.

① What he has told them (mean / means) a lot to me.

② Listening to good songs (make / makes) you relaxed.

③ Keeping promises (is / are) important.

B 다음 사진을 보고 빈칸에 알맞은 단어를 쓰시오.

① The half of the

_____ _____ eaten.

② The half of the

_____ _____ eaten.

C 다음 우리말을 참고하여 빈칸을 채우시오.

① 그 학생들의 3분의 2는 영어를 좋아한다.

Two thirds of _____.

② 부자들은 만일의 경우를 대비해 돈을 저축한다.

The _____ for a rainy day.

③ 그 학급의 학생 숫자는 증가했다.

_____ in the class _____.

A. 다음 괄호 안에서 어법상 알맞은 단어를 고르시오.

① Each answer (is / are) worth 10 points.

② Physics (is / are) one of my favorite subjects.

③ Fifty dollars (is / are) better than nothing.

④ Bread and butter (is / are) good for breakfast.

⑤ There (is / are) a number of people on the street.

⑥ Linguistics (is / are) a study of languages.

⑦ *Romeo and Juliet* (is / are) a sad story.

⑧ Two miles (is / are) a long distance to walk.

⑨ What he has told them (mean / means) a lot to me.

⑩ Listening to good songs (make / makes) you relaxed.

⑪ Keeping promises (is / are) important.

B. 다음 밑줄 친 단어를 어법상 알맞게 고치시오.

⑫ The rich is not always happy.   _____

⑬ The number of people have increased.   _____

⑭ Half of the apple were rotten.   _____

시제 일치와 예외

혼공개념   시제 일치의 법칙 #1

1 주절의 시제가 현재일 때 종속절에 모든 시제 가능

He says that 현재	his parents are at home.
	his parents were at home.
	his parents will be at home.

혼공개념   시제 일치의 법칙 #2

1 주절의 시제가 과거일 때 종속절에 과거, 과거완료 가능

He said that 과거	his parent were at home.
	he had bought the DVD.
	his mom would get well soon.

혼공 팁

시제 일치의 법칙 #2는 다음과 같은 문장으로 고쳐서 이해할 수 있다.

예 He said, "My parents are at home." ⇒ He said that his parents were at home.

혼공개념   시제 일치의 예외란?

1 법칙 #2와 다르게 종속절의 시제가 쓰일 때

1) 현재의 습관이나 사실   ⇒ He said that he goes to bed at 11 every day.

2) 불변의 진리   ⇒ The teacher explained that the Earth is round.

3) 과학적 사실   ⇒ He said that water boils at 100℃.

4) 속담이나 격언   ⇒ They said that time is money.

5) 역사적 사실   ⇒ I knew that Columbus discovered America.

                        ⇒ Dr. Kim said that Felix Hoffman invented aspirin in 1899.

혼공 연습

 주어진 우리말을 참고하여 빈칸을 채우시오.

① He says that his parents _____ at home.
(그의 부모님은 집에 계셨다.)

② He says that his parents _____ at home.
(그의 부모님은 집에 계신다.)

③ He says that his parents _____ at home.
(그의 부모님은 집에 계실 것이다.)

④ He said that his parents _____ at home.
(그의 부모님은 집에 계신다.)

⑤ He said that he _____ the DVD.
(그 DVD를 샀었다.)

⑥ He said that his mom _____ well soon.
(그의 엄마가 곧 회복할 것이다.)

 괄호 안에 들어갈 단어 중 어법상 알맞은 것을 고르시오.

① He said that he (goes / went) to bed at 11 every day.

② The teacher explained that the Earth (is / was) round.

③ He said that water (boils / boiled) at 100℃.

④ They said that time (is / was) money.

⑤ I knew that Columbus (discovers / discovered) America.

⑥ Dr. Kim said that Felix Hoffman (invents / invented) aspirin in 1899.

다음 우리말과 일치하도록 밑줄 친 부분을 어법에 맞게 고쳐 쓰시오.

① 그녀는 매일 10시에 잔다고 나에게 말했다.

She told me that she <u>went</u> to bed at 10 every day.

_____

② 내 부모님께서 나에게 새 스마트 폰을 사주겠다고 약속하셨다.

My parents <u>promises</u> that they <u>will buy</u> me a new smartphone.

_____

③ 그는 나에게 해가 동쪽에서 뜬다고 말했다.

He told me that the sun <u>rose</u> in the east.

_____

 다음 우리말과 일치하도록 괄호 안의 단어 중 알맞은 것을 선택하시오.

① 나는 그녀가 그 선물을 좋아할 거라고 생각했다.

I thought that she (will / would) like the gift.

② 나의 부모님들께서는 내가 1등상을 받을 것이라고 생각하셨다.

My parents thought that I (will / would) win the first prize.

③ 오늘 여러분들은 지구가 태양 주위를 돈다는 것을 배웠습니다.

Today, you learned that the Earth (moves / moved) around the Sun.

A. 다음 괄호 안에서 어법상 알맞은 단어를 고르시오.

① He said that he (goes / went) to bed at 11 every day.

② The teacher explained that the Earth (is / was) round.

③ He said that water (boils / boiled) at 100℃.

④ They said that time (is / was) money.

⑤ I knew that Columbus (discovers / discovered) America.

⑥ Dr. Kim said that Felix Hoffman (invents / invented) aspirin in 1899.

B. 다음 문장의 밑줄 친 부분을 어법상 올바르게 고치고 우리말로 해석하시오.

⑦ She told me that she <u>went</u> to bed at 10 every day.

_____ _____

⑧ He told me that the sun <u>rose</u> in the east.

_____ _____

⑨ Today, you learned that the Earth <u>moved</u> around the Sun.

_____ _____

정답 ① goes ② is ③ boils ④ is ⑤ discovered ⑥ invented ⑦ goes, 그녀는 매일 10시에 잔다고 나에게 말했다. ⑧ rises, 그는 나에게 해가 동쪽에서 뜬다고 말했다. ⑨ moves, 오늘 여러분들은(당신은) 지구가 태양 주위를 돈다는 것을 배웠습니다.

기타 조동사

1 기타 조동사: can, must, will 등의 조동사 이외의 조동사

기타 조동사	의미
used to	~하곤 했다(과거의 규칙 습관)
would	~하곤 했다(과거의 불규칙 습관)
would rather	차라리 ~하는 게 낫다(선택)
would like to	~하고 싶다
had better	~하는 게 낫다 (충고)

예 I used to get up at six.

There used to be a bakery on the hill.

He would fish for trout in this stream.

They would play baseball with me all day long.

They would rather stay home.

You'd rather not go there by yourself.

I would like to have one iced Americano.

You had better listen to his advice.

You'd better not stay here.

혼공 팁

used to와 모양이 비슷한 be used to ~ing, be used to 동사원형을 잘 구분해야 한다.

예 I am used to getting up at six.

The machine is used to cure patients.

Part 1

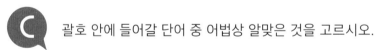
혼공 연습

A 다음 빈칸에 들어갈 조동사 또는 우리말 의미를 적으시오.

기타 조동사	의미
	~하곤 했다(과거의 규칙 습관)
	~하곤 했다(과거의 불규칙 습관)
would rather	
would like to	
	~하는 게 낫다 (충고)

B 어법상 <u>잘못된</u> 한 단어를 찾아 밑줄 긋고 바르게 고치시오.

① They would rather stayed home. _____

② There used to was a bakery. _____

③ He would fishing for trout in this stream. _____

④ They would played baseball with me. _____

C 괄호 안에 들어갈 단어 중 어법상 알맞은 것을 고르시오.

① I used to (get / getting) up at six.

② I am used to (get / getting) up at six.

③ There used to (be / being) a bakery on the hill.

④ The machine is used to (cure / curing) patients.

A 다음 우리말과 뜻이 같도록 빈칸에 알맞은 말을 <보기>에서 골라 쓰시오.

> <보기>　　used to / had better / would / would rather / would like to

① 그는 축구 선수였다(지금은 아니다).

He ＿＿＿＿＿＿＿＿＿＿ be a soccer player.

② 그는 그의 부모님이 말씀하신 것에 귀 기울이는 게 낫다.

He ＿＿＿＿＿＿＿＿＿＿ listen to what his parents said.

③ 저는 차가운 어떤 것을 마시고 싶습니다.

I ＿＿＿＿＿＿＿＿＿＿ drink something cold.

④ 나는 차라리 오늘 그 책을 반납하는 게 낫겠다.

I ＿＿＿＿＿＿＿＿＿＿ return the book today.

B 다음 괄호 안에 주어진 말들을 올바른 순서로 배열하시오.

① He (had / not / go / better / swimming) today.

＿＿＿＿＿＿＿＿＿＿＿＿＿＿＿＿＿＿＿＿＿＿＿＿＿＿＿＿＿＿＿

② I would like (raise / to / hamsters / at home / a few).

＿＿＿＿＿＿＿＿＿＿＿＿＿＿＿＿＿＿＿＿＿＿＿＿＿＿＿＿＿＿＿

C 다음 사진을 보고, 괄호 안의 단어를 이용하여 영작하시오.

There used ＿＿＿＿＿＿＿＿＿＿＿＿＿＿＿＿＿＿＿＿.

(a palace)

A. 다음 빈칸을 예시처럼 채우시오.

기타 조동사	의미
used to	~하곤 했다(과거의 규칙 습관)
	~하곤 했다(과거의 불규칙 습관)
	차라리 ~하는 게 낫다(선택)
	~하고 싶다
	~하는 게 낫다 (충고)

B. 다음 문장들을 우리말로 해석하시오.

① You'd rather not go there by yourself.

_____

② They would play baseball with me.

_____

③ I would like to drink something cold.

_____

④ You had better listen to his advice.

_____

C. 다음 우리말을 참고하여 영작하시오.

⑤ 나는 6시에 일어나곤 했었다(지금은 아니다).

_____

⑥ 언덕 위에 빵집이 있었다(지금은 없다).

_____

⑦ 그는 송어를 잡으려고 이 개울에서 낚시를 하곤 했다(불규칙).

_____

⑧ 그는 오늘 수영하러 가지 않는 게 낫겠다(충고).

_____

정답 A의 정답은 앞 페이지의 오늘 공부했던 박스를 참고하세요. ① 너는 차라리 거기에 혼자 가지 않는 편이 낫겠다. ② 그들은 나와 야구를 하곤 했었다. ③ 나는 차가운 어떤 것을 마시고 싶다. ④ 너는 그의 충고를 듣는 게 낫다. ⑤ I used to get up at six. ⑥ There used to be a bakery on the hill. ⑦ He would fish for trout in this stream. ⑧ He had better not go swimming today.

조동사 + have + p.p.

> 🔵 **혼공개념** 조동사 + have + p.p.

1 과거의 사건이나 상태에 대한 언급을 할 때 사용됨

  예 He <u>must be</u> serious. (현재)

  He <u>must have been</u> serious. (과거)

> 🔵 **혼공개념** 조동사 + have + p.p.의 다양한 용법들

1 must + have + p.p. (강한 추측: 분명히 ~했을 것이다)

  예 He <u>must have known</u> her phone number.

  They <u>must have finished</u> their homework.

2 should + have + p.p. (후회: ~했어야만 했다)

  예 She <u>should have gone</u> home.

  John <u>should have been</u> more careful.

3 cannot + have + p.p. (부정적 추측: ~이었을 리가 없다)

  예 Denise <u>cannot have eaten</u> all the food.

  The boy <u>cannot have been</u> a student.

  혼공 팁

  could have p.p.는 '~할 수도 있었을 텐데'라는 의미로도 쓰임

  cf) It <u>could have been</u> much better.

4 may(might) + have + p.p. (약한 추측: ~이었을런지도 모른다)

  예 She <u>may(might) have forgotten</u> to call me.

  Justin <u>may(might) have been</u> gloomy.

Part 1

혼공 연습

A 다음 표현을 '조동사 + have + p.p.'의 형태로 고치시오.

① must be   _____

② must finish   _____

③ should be   _____

④ should go   _____

⑤ may forget   _____

B 다음 우리말과 일치하도록 빈칸에 알맞은 표현을 <보기>에서 찾아서 쓰시오.

<보기>   must have   should have   cannot have   could have   might have

① 그것은 훨씬 더 나을 수도 있었을 텐데.

It _____ been much better.

② Denise가 모든 음식을 다 먹었을 리 없다.

Denise _____ eaten all the food.

③ John은 더 조심했어야만 했다.

John _____ been more careful.

④ 그는 그녀의 전화번호를 알고 있었음이 틀림없다.

He _____ known her phone number.

⑤ 그녀는 나에게 전화할 것을 잊었을런지도 모른다.

She _____ forgotten to call me.

A 우리말과 일치하도록 빈칸에 주어진 단어를 활용하여 알맞은 표현을 쓰시오.

① Jun이 캐나다에 머물렀던 것이 틀림없다.

Jun _____ in Canada. (stay)

② 너는 변기에 물을 내렸어야 한다.

You _____ the toilet. (flush)

③ 그는 거기서 Jim을 만났을 리가 없다.

He _____ Jim there. (meet)

④ 그의 이야기는 사실이었을런지도 모른다.

His story _____ true. (be)

B 다음 괄호 안에서 알맞은 조동사를 고르시오.

① I have just missed the flight. I (should / may) have left home earlier.

② He is a very honest student. It (can't / must) have been his fault.

③ Oh, it's raining outside. I (should / must) have brought my umbrella.

C 다음은 오늘 Jenny가 시험을 친 뒤 쓴 일기의 일부분이다. 빈칸에 적절한 표현들을 쓰시오.

Last week, I _____ (sleep) too much.

I think I _____ (study) harder for this exam.

A. 다음 표현을 '조동사 + have + p.p.'의 형태로 고치시오.

① must be   _____

② must finish   _____

③ should be   _____

④ should go   _____

⑤ may forget   _____

B. 다음 우리말을 참고하여 빈칸을 채우시오.

⑥ Denise는 모든 음식을 다 먹었을 리가 없다.

Denise _____ all the food.

⑦ John은 더 조심했어야만 했다.

John _____ more careful.

⑧ 그는 그녀의 전화번호를 알고 있었음이 틀림없다.

He _____.

⑨ 그녀는 나에게 전화할 것을 잊었을런지도 모른다.

She _____.

⑩ 그는 거기서 Jim을 만났을 리가 없다.

He _____ there.

⑪ 나는 내 우산을 가져왔어야 했다.

I _____.

정답 ① must have been ② must have finished ③ should have been ④ should have gone ⑤ may have forgotten ⑥ can't(cannot) have eaten ⑦ should have been ⑧ must have known her phone number ⑨ may(might) have forgotten to call me ⑩ can't(cannot) have met Jim ⑪ should have brought my umbrella

현재완료진행형 / 수동태

1 현재완료진행형: 과거부터 지금까지 연결되는 동작을 표현하고, 지금도 진행 중이라는 것을 강조함

현재완료	have + p.p.
진행형	+ be + ~ing
	have + been + ~ing

    I have + p.p.
    +   be   + studying
─────────────────────
    I have   been   studying.

[예] He has repaired the car. (현재완료)

He has been repairing the car. (현재완료진행)

1 현재완료수동태: 과거부터 지금까지 어떤 동작의 영향을 받고 있는 상황

현재완료	have + p.p.
수동태	+ be + p.p.
	have + been + p.p.

    The problems   have   p.p.
      +   be   + solved
─────────────────────
The problems   have been   solved.

[예] He has been chosen as a leader.

A new building has been built by the company.

A 다음 문장을 괄호 안의 지시대로 바꾸어 쓰시오.

① He repairs the car. (현재완료)

_____

② He repairs the car. (현재완료진행)

_____

③ The problems solve. (현재완료수동)

_____

④ He chooses as a leader. (현재완료수동)

_____

⑤ A new building builds by the company. (현재완료수동)

_____

B 다음 괄호 안에서 어법상 알맞은 것을 고르시오.

① He has been (repairing / repaired) the car.

② The problems have been (solving / solved).

③ He has been (choosing / chosen) as a leader.

④ A new building has been (building / built) by the company.

C 다음 문장에서 어법상 잘못된 한 단어를 찾아 밑줄 긋고 바르게 고치시오.

① He has been waited for three hours.

_____

② The scientist has been worked on an important project.

_____

③ A lot of buildings have been destroying by the tornado.

_____

A 다음 사진을 보고 빈칸에 알맞은 현재완료진행형을 쓰시오.

① She _____ books for two hours.

② He _____ the car.

③ They _____ about the topic.

B 우리말과 일치하도록 현재완료진행 또는 수동을 사용하여 다음 빈칸을 채우시오.

① 내 아빠는 9시 이후로 계속해서 TV를 쭉 보고 계신다.

My dad _____ TV _____ 9 o'clock.

② Chloe는 2시간째 계속해서 울고 있다.

Chloe _____ for two _____.

③ 그 컴퓨터는 한 시간 동안 계속해서 수리되었다.

The computer _____ for an hour.

C 다음 질문에 알맞은 대답을 완성하시오.

A: How long have you been studying English?

B: I _____ for _____.

A. 다음 괄호 안에서 어법상 알맞은 것을 고르시오.

① He has been (repairing / repaired) the car.

② The problems have been (solving / solved).

③ He has been (choosing / chosen) as a leader.

④ A new building has been (building / built) by the company.

⑤ I have been (studying / studied) for 2 hours.

⑥ The scientist has been (working / worked) on an important project.

⑦ A lot of buildings have been (destroying / destroyed) by the tornado.

B. 다음 문장들을 우리말로 해석하시오.

⑧ She has been reading books for 2 hours.

_____

⑨ They have been talking about the topic.

_____

⑩ The computer has been fixed for 1 hour.

_____

⑪ I have been studying English for 10 years.

_____

정답 ① repairing ② solved ③ chosen ④ built ⑤ studying ⑥ working ⑦ destroyed ⑧ 그녀는 2시간 동안 계속해서 독서를 하고 있는 중이
다. ⑨ 그들은 그 주제에 관해 계속해서 이야기하고 있는 중이다. ⑩ 그 컴퓨터는 한 시간 동안 계속해서 수리되고 있다. ⑪ 나는 영어를 10년 동안 계
속해서 공부하고 있는 중이다.

조동사 + be + p.p.

혼공개념 | 조동사 + be + p.p.의 개념

1 조동사의 의미에 수동태(be + p.p.)를 더한 것

조동사	can, will, must, should...
수동태 +	be + p.p.
	조동사 + be + p.p.

must
+ is + done
must be done(반드시 행해져야 한다)

예 Your job <u>must be done</u> by 1 p.m. (+ 의무)

The full moon <u>can be seen</u> in my yard. (+ 가능)

혼공개념 | 수동태 + by 이외의 전치사

1 수동태 뒤에 by가 자주 나오지만, 그 이외의 전치사를 택하기도 함

표현	의미
be known to	~에게 알려져 있다(대상)
be known for	~로 알려지다(이유)
be known by	~로 알 수 있다(판단 기준)
be known as	~로서 알려져 있다(자격)

예 My friend, Kevin, <u>is known to</u> everybody.

The restaurant <u>is known for</u> its spaghetti.

A man <u>is known by</u> the company he keeps.

He <u>is known as</u> a lawyer.

A 주어진 조동사를 넣어 다음 문장을 다시 쓰시오.

① Your job is done by 1 p.m. (must)

_____

② The full moon is seen in my yard. (can)

_____

③ This puzzle is solved by a famous professor. (will)

_____

④ All of my classmates are invited to my birthday party. (will)

_____

B 다음 괄호 안에 알맞은 전치사를 쓰시오.

① My friend, Kevin, is known _____ everybody. (대상)

② The restaurant is known _____ its spaghetti. (이유)

③ A man is known _____ the company he keeps. (판단)

④ He is known _____ a lawyer. (자격)

C 다음 문장을 수동태로 만드시오.

① Smoke filled our room.

_____

② My test score satisfied my parents.

_____

③ The news surprised us.

_____

A 다음 <보기>의 표현을 각각 한 번만 활용하여 문장을 완성하시오.

<보기>	do	discuss	save	plant	see	hand in

① More money should _____ for a rainy day.

② The rainbow can _____ from the balcony.

③ The topic will _____ at the meeting.

④ Something must _____ right away.

⑤ Your assignment must _____ by Friday.

⑥ Some flowers will _____ in the garden.

B 다음 우리말과 일치하도록 빈칸에 알맞은 전치사를 쓰시오.

① 그녀의 아름다움은 세상에 알려져 있다.

= Her beauty is known _____ the world.

② Gordon Ramsay는 그의 요리 기술로 알려져 있다.

= Gordon Ramsay is known _____ his cooking skills.

③ Jimmy는 열심히 일하는 사람으로 알려져 있다.

= Jimmy is known _____ a hard worker.

④ 나무는 그것의 열매로 알 수 있다.

= A tree is known _____ its fruits.

C 다음 우리말과 일치하도록 빈칸에 알맞은 단어를 쓰시오.

① 당신은 나의 제안에 흥미가 있나요?

= Are you _____ _____ my suggestion?

② 그는 내 여동생과 5월에 결혼할 것이다.

= He will be _____ _____ my sister in May.

③ 나는 희망으로 가득 차 있었다.

= I _____ _____ _____ hope.

A. 다음 빈칸을 예시처럼 채우시오.

표현	의미
be known to	~에게 알려져 있다(대상)
	~로 알려지다(이유)
	~로 알 수 있다(판단 기준)
	~로서 알려져 있다(자격)

B. 주어진 조동사를 넣어 다음 문장을 다시 쓰시오.

① Your job is done by 1 p.m. (must)

_____

② The full moon is seen in my yard. (can)

_____

③ This puzzle is solved by a famous professor. (will)

_____

C. 다음 문장들을 우리말로 해석하시오.

④ The topic will be discussed at the meeting.

_____

⑤ Gordon Ramsay is known for his cooking skills.

_____

⑥ Something must be done right away.

_____

⑦ Are you interested in my suggestion?

_____

정답   A의 정답은 앞 페이지의 오늘 공부했던 박스를 참고하세요.   ① Your job must be done by 1 p.m.   ② The full moon can be seen in my yard.
③ This puzzle will be solved by a famous professor.   ④ 그 주제는 회의에서 논의되어질 것이다.   ⑤ Gordon Ramsay는 그의 요리 기술로 알려져 있다.
⑥ 어떤 것이 즉시 행해져야만 한다.   ⑦ 당신은 나의 제안에 관심이 있으신가요?

화법 전환

💡 혼공개념 직접화법 VS 간접화법

1 직접화법: 어떤 사람이 한 말을 큰 따옴표 " " 안에 그대로 옮긴 것

2 간접화법: 어떤 사람이 한 말을 남이 대신 옮겨 전달하는 것

직접화법 ⇒ 간접화법	
She said, "I need some help."	She said that she needed some help.
She said to me, "I will help you."	She told me that she would help me.

💡 혼공개념 의문문의 화법 전환

1 의문사가 있는 의문문: 전달 동사를 ask로 바꾸고 뒤에 간접의문문 '의문사 + 주어 + 동사'를 씀

2 의문사가 없는 의문문: 전달 동사를 ask로 바꾸고 뒤에 간접의문문 'if(whether) + 주어 + 동사'를 씀

직접화법 ⇒ 간접화법	
He said to me, "What is your name?"	He asked me what my name was.
He said to me, "Do you know Tyler?"	He asked me if(whether) I knew Tyler.

💡 혼공개념 명령문의 화법 전환

1 방법: 전달 동사를 tell, order, advise, ask 등으로 바꾸고 뒤에 '목적어 + to부정사'를 씀

직접화법 ⇒ 간접화법	
Mom said to me, "Study hard."	Mom told me to study hard.

💡 혼공개념 기타 화법 전환

1 감탄문: 전달 동사를 cry, exclaim, shout로 바꿈

2 청유문: 전달 동사를 suggest로 바꾸고 뒤에 that we + (should) + 동사원형으로 씀

직접화법 ⇒ 간접화법	
She said, "How handsome he is!"	She shouted how handsome he was.
Jason said, "Let's eat."	Jason suggested that we (should) eat.

혼공 연습

A 다음 중 직접화법인 것은 '직접', 간접화법인 것은 '간접'이라 쓰시오.

① She told me that she would help me.   _____

② He said to me, "What is your name?"   _____

③ Mom told me to study hard.   _____

④ Jason said, "Let's eat."   _____

B 직접화법을 간접화법으로 고칠 때 빈칸에 알맞은 단어를 쓰시오.

① She said, "I need some help."

→ She said that _____ _____ some help.

② She said to me, "I will help you."

→ She _____ me that _____ _____ help _____.

③ He said to me, "What is your name?"

→ He _____ me what _____ name _____.

④ He said to me, "Do you know Tyler?"

→ He asked me _____ I _____ Tyler.

⑤ Mom said to me, "Study hard."

→ Mom told me _____ _____ hard.

⑥ Jason said, "Let's eat."

→ Jason _____ that we _____ eat.

A 괄호 안에서 알맞은 단어를 고른 뒤, 빈칸을 채워 간접화법을 완성하시오.

① Jessica (said / told), "I am really tired."

→ Jessica (said / told) that _____ _____ really tired.

② She (said / told) to me, "I don't like the color."

→ She (said / told) me that _____ _____ _____ the color.

③ They (said / told), "We want to go on a picnic."

→ They (said / told) that _____ _____ to go on a picnic.

B 다음 괄호 안에서 알맞은 단어를 고르시오.

① Dad told me (if / to) stop playing computer games.

② I (shouted / said) what an exciting game it was.

③ Ken (said to / told) me to calm down.

④ My family doctor told my mom (to not / not to) drink coffee.

C 밑줄 친 부분 중 잘못된 한 단어를 찾아 바르게 고치시오.

He said to me, "I will solve the problem."

= He told me that I would solve the problem.

_____ → _____

A. 다음 괄호 안에서 알맞은 단어를 고르시오.

① Dad told me (if / to) stop playing computer games.

② I (shouted / said) what an exciting game it was.

③ Ken (said to / told) me to calm down.

④ My family doctor told my mom (to not / not to) drink coffee.

B. 직접화법을 간접화법으로 고칠 때 빈칸에 알맞은 표현을 쓰시오.

⑤ She said, "I need some help."

　　She said that _____.

⑥ He said to me, "What is your name?"

　　He _____.

⑦ He said to me, "Do you know Tyler?"

　　He asked _____.

⑧ Mom said to me, "Study hard."

　　Mom told me _____.

가정법 과거

1 가정법 과거: 현재 사실과 완전히 반대되는 상황을 가정하거나, 가능성이 없는 상상을 할 때 쓰는 표현법

2 방법: If 주어 were / 과거동사 ~, 주어 + 조동사의 과거형 + 동사원형 ~

주어가 ~한다면   주어가 ~ 텐데

예 If I were you, I wouldn't go there.

If I had a lot of money, I could buy you a nice car.

If I were a bird, I could fly to you.

If I won the lottery, I would go to New York.

혼공개념 단순 조건문 VS 가정법 과거

1 단순 조건문: 사실 여부를 파악할 수 없음

예 If she is diligent, I will hire her.

(그녀가 근면한지 아닌지 알 수 없음)

2 가정법 과거: 현재 사실과 반대됨

예 If she were diligent, I would hire her.

(평소 그녀는 근면하지 않은 사람임)

혼공 팁

※ 현대 영어에서는 If she was diligent, ~~ 처럼 was를 써서 가정법 과거를 나타내기도 한다.

A 다음 괄호 안에서 알맞은 것을 고르시오.

① If Jun (is / were) my boyfriend, I would do whatever he wants.

② If she (is / were) diligent, I would hire her.

③ What would happen if there (are / were) no police officers?

B 다음 밑줄 친 부분을 가정법 과거로 바꾸어 쓰시오.

① If I <u>am</u> you, I <u>won't go</u> there.

_____, _____

② If I <u>have</u> a lot of money, I <u>can buy</u> you a nice car.

_____, _____

③ If I <u>am</u> a bird, I <u>can fly</u> to you.

_____, _____

④ If I <u>win</u> the lottery, I <u>will go</u> to New York.

_____, _____

C 다음 문장을 가정법 과거로 바꿀 때 빈칸을 채우시오.

① As he doesn't tell me the truth, I don't trust him.

→ If he _____ me the truth, I _____ trust him.

② Since this food is cold, it doesn't taste good.

→ If this food _____ cold, it would taste good.

A 다음 사진을 보고 빈칸을 채우시오.

① If I won the lottery,

I _____ to Australia.

② If I won the lottery,

I _____ some money.

B 다음 우리말과 일치하도록 빈칸을 채우시오.

① 내가 그라면, 그녀에게 데이트 신청을 하지 않을 텐데.

→ If I _____ him, I _____ _____ her out. (ask out)

② 내가 시골에 산다면, 새를 보러 더 자주 갈 텐데.

→ If I _____ in the countryside, I _____ go bird watching more often.

C 다음 문장을 가정법 과거로 옮기시오.

① It is cold outside, so we can't go on a picnic.

_____

② I don't have a camera, so I can't take a picture of you.

_____

혼공
복습

A. 다음 괄호 안에서 알맞은 것을 고르시오.

① If Jun (is / were) my boyfriend, I would do whatever he wants.

② What would happen if there (are / were) no police officers?

B. 다음 밑줄 친 부분을 가정법 과거로 바꾸어 쓰시오.

③ If I am you, I won't go there.

_____, _____

④ If I have a lot of money, I can buy you a nice car.

_____, _____

⑤ If I win the lottery, I will go to New York.

_____, _____

C. 다음 우리말과 같도록 빈칸을 채우시오.

⑥ 내가 그라면, 그녀에게 데이트 신청을 하지 않을 텐데.

If I _____ him, I _____ _____ her out. (ask out)

⑦ 내가 시골에 산다면, 새를 보러 더 자주 갈 텐데.

If I _____ in the countryside, I _____ go bird watching more often.

가정법 과거완료

1 단순 조건문: 상황에 대해 사실 여부를 알 수 없을 때 씀

　　예 If she is diligent, I will hire her.

　　⇒ 그녀가 근면한지 알 수 없음

2 가정법 과거: 현재 사실에 반대되는 상황을 표현

　　예 If she were diligent, I would hire her.

　　⇒ 내가 아는 현재의 그녀는 절대 근면하지 않음

3 가정법 과거완료: 과거 사실에 반대되는 상황을 표현

　　예 If she had been diligent, I would have hired her.

　　⇒ 내가 아는 예전의 그녀는 절대 근면하지 않았음

혼공개념 가정법 과거완료

1 방법: If 주어 had + p.p. ~, 　주어 + 조동사의 과거형 + have + p.p. ~

　　　　　주어가 ~했었다면,　　　　　　　　주어가 ~ 했을 텐데

　　예 If I had brought my homework, my teacher would have been pleased.

　　　= I didn't bring my homework, so my teacher was not pleased.

　　If she had not been tired, she could have won the speech contest.

　　　= She was tired, so she couldn't win the speech contest.

　　If I had gotten up earlier, I could have caught the first train.

　　　= I didn't get up earlier, so I couldn't catch the first train.

A 다음 밑줄 친 부분을 가정법 과거완료로 고치시오.

① If she <u>is diligent</u>, I <u>will hire</u> her.

_____

② If I <u>were a bird</u>, I <u>could fly</u> to you.

_____

③ If I <u>studied harder</u>, I <u>could be</u> a scientist.

_____

B 다음 우리말 의미를 참고해서 빈칸을 채우시오.

① 그녀가 근면한지 알 수 없음

If she _____ diligent, I _____ hire her.

② 내가 아는 현재의 그녀는 절대 근면하지 않음

If she _____ diligent, I _____ hire her.

③ 내가 아는 예전의 그녀는 절대 근면하지 않았음

If she _____ diligent, I _____ her.

C 다음 문장을 가정법 과거완료로 바꿀 때, 빈칸을 채우시오.

① I didn't bring my homework, so I called my mom.
  ⇒ If I _____ my homework, I _____ called my mom.

② She made a few mistakes, so she couldn't win the speech contest.
  ⇒ If she _____ a few mistakes, she could _____ the speech contest.

③ I didn't get up earlier, so I couldn't catch the train.
  ⇒ If I _____ earlier, I _____ the train.

A 다음 괄호 안에서 어법상 알맞은 것을 고르시오.

① If I (knew / had known) Lily better, I wouldn't have asked her to do it.

② If you (were / had been) there, you could have seen the actor.

③ If Kevin had come to my party, he would (see / have seen) my girlfriend.

④ If she had known the truth, she would (tell / have told) me about it.

B 다음 괄호 안에 주어진 단어들을 올바른 순서로 배열하시오.

① If our kids had been thirsty,
(to / would / drink / have / given / I / them / something).

_____

② If he had run a little faster, (have / race / won / could / he / the).

_____

③ If (tired / not / I / had / been), I could have stayed up all night.

_____

C 다음 문장을 보고, 빈칸을 채우시오.

① As I didn't eat anything, I was hungry.
⇒ If I _____ anything, I _____ been hungry.

② Since she didn't study hard, she failed the test.
⇒ If she _____ hard, she wouldn't have _____ the test.

A. 다음 우리말 의미를 참고해서 빈칸을 채우시오.

① 그녀가 근면한지 알 수 없음

If she _____ diligent, I _____ hire her.

② 내가 아는 현재의 그녀는 절대 근면하지 않음

If she _____ diligent, I _____ hire her.

③ 내가 아는 예전의 그녀는 절대 근면하지 않았음

If she _____ diligent, I _____ her.

B. 다음 괄호 안에서 어법상 알맞은 것을 고르시오.

④ If I (knew / had known) Lily better, I wouldn't have asked her to do it.

⑤ If Kevin had come to my party, he would (see / have seen) my girlfriend.

⑥ If she had known the truth, she would (tell / have told) me about it.

C. 다음 괄호 안에 주어진 단어들을 올바른 순서로 배열하시오.

⑦ If our kids had been thirsty,

(to / would / drink / have / given / I / them / something).

_____

⑧ If he had run a little faster, (have / race / won / could / he / the).

_____

I wish 가정법

1 I wish 가정법 과거: 현재 이루기 힘든 소망에 대해 말할 때 씀

2 방법: 'I wish + 주어 + were / 과거동사 ~'

내가 ~한다면(하다면) 좋을 텐데

[예] I wish I were taller than you.

= I am sorry I am not taller than you.

1 I wish 가정법 과거완료: 과거에 이루기 힘들었던 소망에 대해 말할 때 씀

2 방법: 'I wish + 주어 + had + been / p.p. ~'

내가 ~했었다면 좋았을 텐데

[예] I wish I had gotten superpowers.

= I am sorry I didn't get superpowers.

혼공 팁

I wish 가정법 과거와 과거완료의 시제 차이를 잘 이해해야 한다.

[예] I wish I were rich. (현재 부자이기를 바람)

I wish I had been rich. (과거에 부자였기를 바람)

I wish I spoke French fluently. (현재 잘하기를 바람)

I wish I had spoken French fluently. (과거에 잘했기를 바람)

혼공 연습

A 다음 문장을 괄호 안의 지시대로 바꾸어 쓰시오.

① I wish I am taller than you. (가정법 과거)

_____

② I wish I got superpowers. (가정법 과거완료)

_____

③ I wish I were rich. (가정법 과거완료)

_____

④ I wish I spoke French fluently. (가정법 과거완료)

_____

B 다음 우리말 의미와 주어진 단어를 참고하여 빈칸을 채우시오.

① 현재 부자이기를 바람   I wish I _____ rich. (be)

② 과거에 부자였기를 바람   I wish I _____ rich. (be)

③ 현재 잘하기를 바람   I wish I _____ French fluently. (speak)

④ 과거에 잘했기를 바람   I wish I _____ French fluently. (speak)

C 다음 우리말로 된 가정법 부분을 영어로 옮기시오.

① I wish 내가 그녀 보다 키가 더 컸었기를.

= I wish I _____.

② I wish 내가 그 대회에서 우승했었기를.

= I wish I _____.

다음 괄호 안에서 알맞은 것을 고르시오.

① I don't like taking a bus. I wish I (had / had had) my own car.

② I wish I (did / had done) my homework last night.

③ We couldn't go on a picnic on that day.
I wish it (didn't rain / hadn't rained).

B <보기>의 적절한 동사를 골라 빈칸에 알맞은 형태로 바꾸어 쓰시오.

<보기>	travel	be	live

① I wish my grades _____ as good as yours.(가정법 과거)

② I wish I _____ to more countries.(가정법 과거완료)

③ I wish I _____ in a house with a big yard.(가정법 과거완료)

C 사진을 참고하여 가정법 문장을 완성하시오.

① I wish my mom _____
_____ for me. (가정법 과거)

② I wish I _____
the marathon. (가정법 과거완료)

A. 다음 밑줄 친 부분을 지시대로 고치시오.

① I wish I <u>am taller</u> than you. (가정법 과거)

_____

② I wish I <u>got</u> superpowers. (가정법 과거완료)

_____

③ I wish I <u>were</u> rich. (가정법 과거완료)

_____

④ I wish I <u>spoke</u> French fluently. (가정법 과거완료)

_____

B. 다음 우리말로 된 가정법 부분을 영어로 옮기시오.

⑤ I wish <u>내가 그녀 보다 키가 더 컸었기를.</u>

　= I wish I _____ than her.

⑥ I wish <u>내가 그 대회에서 우승했었기를.</u>

　= I wish I _____ the contest.

C. 다음 괄호 안에서 알맞은 것을 고르시오.

⑦ I don't like taking a bus. I wish I (had / had had) my own car.
⑧ We couldn't go on a picnic on that day. I wish it (didn't rain / hadn't rained).

정답　① were taller　② had got(gotten)　③ had been　④ had spoken　⑤ had been taller　⑥ had won　⑦ had　⑧ hadn't rained

as if 가정법

혼공개념 as if 가정법 과거란?

1 as if 가정법 과거: 현재 사실과 반대되는 일을 가정할 때 사용함

2 방법: 주어 + 동작 + as if 주어 + were / 과거동사 ~
      ~가 ~ 한다   마치 ~가 ~인 것처럼

예 He talks as if he were Steve Jobs.

   = In fact, he is not Steve Jobs.

   She talks as if she were a billionaire.

   = In fact, she is not a billionaire.

혼공개념 as if 가정법 과거완료란?

1 as if 가정법 과거완료: 과거 사실과 반대되는 일을 가정할 때 사용함

2 방법: 주어 + 동작 + as if 주어 + had been / p.p. ~
      ~가 ~ 한다   마치 ~가 ~이었던 것처럼

예 Cathy talks as if she had watched the movie.

   In fact, Cathy didn't watch the movie.

   He talks as if he had met Mr. Park.

   In fact, he didn't meet Mr. Park.

혼공 팁

as if 가정법 과거와 과거완료의 차이를 예문을 통해 확인하자.

예 He talks as if he were rich.(as if 가정법 과거)

   He talks as if he had been rich.(as if 가정법 과거완료)

혼공 연습

A 다음 문장들의 의미가 통하도록 빈칸을 채우시오.

① He talks as if he _____ Steve Jobs.

→ In fact, he is not Steve Jobs.

② Cathy talks as if she _____ the movie.

→ In fact, Cathy didn't watch the movie.

③ She talks as if she were a billionaire.

→ In fact, she _____ a billionaire.

④ He talks as if he had met Mr. Park.

→ In fact, he _____ Mr. Park.

B 다음 우리말과 일치하도록 빈칸을 채우시오.

① 그는 과거에 부자였던 것처럼 말한다.

He talks as if he _____ rich.

② 그는 지금 부자인 것처럼 말한다.

He _____ as if he _____ rich.

③ 그는 과거에 Mr. Park을 만났던 것처럼 말한다.

He _____ as if he _____ Mr. Park.

④ 그는 그가 Steve Jobs였던 것처럼 말한다.

He _____ as if _____ Steve Jobs.

다음 괄호 안에서 내용상 알맞은 것을 고르시오.

① They treat me as if I (were not / were) their customer. This is not fair.

② She talks as if she (saw / had seen) aliens. In fact, she didn't see anything at all.

③ A broken cup was on the table. But he behaves as if nothing (happened / had happened).

β 다음 우리말과 일치하도록 빈칸을 채우시오.

① Jun은 자신이 마치 Gordon Ramsay인 것처럼 말한다.

= Jun _____ as if _____ _____ Gordon Ramsay.

② 내 할아버지는 마치 자신이 10대인 것처럼 말씀하신다.

= My grandfather _____ as if he _____ a teenager.

③ 그녀는 밤중에 한숨도 못 잤던 것처럼 말한다.

= She talks as if she _____ _____ all night.

A. 다음 문장들의 의미가 통하도록 빈칸을 채우시오.

① He talks as if he _____ Steve Jobs.

    → In fact, he is not Steve Jobs.

② He talks as if he had met Mr. Park.

    → In fact, he _____ Mr. Park.

B. 다음 우리말과 일치하도록 빈칸을 채우시오.

③ 그는 과거에 부자였던 것처럼 말한다.

    He talks as if he _____ rich.

④ 그는 지금 부자인 것처럼 말한다.

    He _____ as if he _____ rich.

⑤ Jun은 자신이 마치 Gordon Ramsay인 것처럼 말한다.

    Jun _____ as if _____ _____ Gordon Ramsay.

⑥ 그녀는 밤중에 한숨도 못 잤던 것처럼 말한다.

    She talks as if she _____ _____ all night.

최상급의 표현

🔍 혼공개념 | 최상급이란?

1 최상급: 셋 이상의 대상 중 가장 '~한' 대상을 말할 때 쓰는 용법

2 방법

    1) 형용사 / 부사 + est, st

    2) most + 형용사 / 부사

    예 Ryan is the tallest boy in his class.

       My son runs (the) fastest among the boys.

       Health is the most important thing in my life.

🔍 혼공개념 | 최상급을 나타내는 기타 표현

1 비교급 + than any other + 단수명사: 다른 어떤 ~보다 더 ~한

    예 Seoul is bigger than any other city in South Korea.

       Love is more precious than any other thing.

2 비교급 + than all the other + 복수명사: 모든 다른 ~보다 더 한

    예 Seoul is bigger than all the other cities in South Korea.

       Love is more precious than all the other things.

3 no other + 단수명사 + 비교급 + than: 다른 어떤 ~도 ~보다 ~하지 않은

    예 No other man was taller than Seo Jang-hoon.

4 no other + 단수명사 + as 원급 as: 다른 어떤 ~도 ~만큼 ~하지 않은

    예 No other teacher was as thin as Mr. Heo.

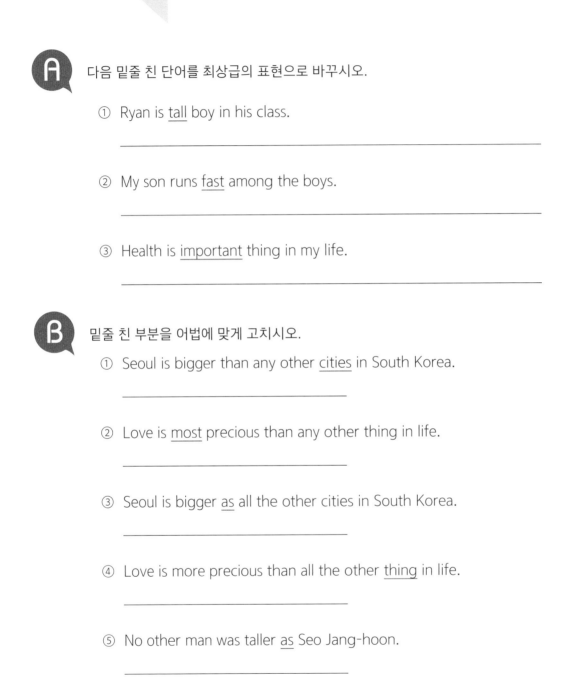

A 다음 밑줄 친 단어를 최상급의 표현으로 바꾸시오.

① Ryan is <u>tall</u> boy in his class.

_____

② My son runs <u>fast</u> among the boys.

_____

③ Health is <u>important</u> thing in my life.

_____

B 밑줄 친 부분을 어법에 맞게 고치시오.

① Seoul is bigger than any other <u>cities</u> in South Korea.

_____

② Love is <u>most</u> precious than any other thing in life.

_____

③ Seoul is bigger <u>as</u> all the other cities in South Korea.

_____

④ Love is more precious than all the other <u>thing</u> in life.

_____

⑤ No other man was taller <u>as</u> Seo Jang-hoon.

_____

⑥ No other <u>teachers were</u> as thin as Mr. Heo.

_____

A 다음 괄호 안에서 어법상 알맞은 것을 고르시오.

① Nothing is as precious (than / as) love.

② Nothing is more important (than / as) passion in learning English.

③ *Interstellar* is the (more / most) wonderful movie of them.

④ I can play the guitar (well / better) than any other student.

⑤ No other (student is / students are) noisier than Tom.

B 다음 괄호 안에 주어진 단어를 이용해 최상급 의미의 문장을 완성하시오.

① Coffee is _____ drink in the world. (popular)

② No other person is as _____ Tom is. (energetic)

③ No other student in our school is as _____ Lily is. (talkative)

C 우리말과 일치하도록 주어진 단어들을 올바르게 배열하시오.

① 어떤 다른 방법도 이것보다 더 비쌀 순 없다.

(expensive / other / no / way / is / this / more / than)

_____

② 어떤 것도 이 참사만큼 나쁠 것이 없었다.

(disaster / bad / nothing / was / as / as / this)

_____

③ 태평양은 세계에서 가장 큰 대양이다.

(largest / the Pacific Ocean / is / ocean / the / in the world)

_____

혼공
복습

A. 밑줄 친 부분을 어법에 맞게 고치시오.

① Seoul is bigger than any other <u>cities</u> in South Korea.

_____

② Love is <u>most</u> precious than any other thing in life.

_____

③ No other <u>teachers were</u> as thin as Mr. Heo.

_____

B. 다음 괄호 안에서 어법상 알맞은 것을 고르시오.

④ Nothing is more important (than / as) passion in learning English.

⑤ _Interstellar_ is the (more / most) wonderful movie of them.

⑥ No other (student is / students are) noisier than Tom.

C. 우리말과 일치하도록 주어진 단어들을 올바르게 배열하시오.

⑦ 어떤 다른 방법도 이것보다 더 비쌀 순 없다.

(expensive / other / no / way / is / this / more / than)

_____

⑧ 어떤 것도 이 참사만큼 나쁠 것이 없었다.

(disaster / bad / nothing / was / as / as / this)

_____

정답 ① city ② more ③ teacher was ④ than ⑤ most ⑥ student is ⑦ No other way is more expensive than this. ⑧ Nothing was as bad as this disaster.

비교급 / 최상급의 관용 표현

 혼공개념 선택의문문이란?

1 선택의문문: 둘 중 하나를 선택하게 하는 질문을 할 때 쓰는 표현

2 의미: A와 B 둘 중에 무엇을 더 ~하는가?

> 예 A: <u>Which</u> season do you like <u>more</u>, summer <u>or</u> winter?
>
> B: I like winter <u>more</u> because I was born in Toronto.
>
> A: <u>Which</u> do you <u>prefer</u>, bus <u>or</u> train?
>
> B: I <u>prefer</u> a train because it makes fewer stops.

 혼공개념 the 비교급, the 비교급

1 의미: ~하면 할수록 더 ~하다

> 예 <u>The worse</u> medicine tastes, <u>the more</u> it works.
>
> <u>The more</u> we learn, <u>the more</u> carefully we should talk.
>
> <u>The more</u> fast food you eat, <u>the fatter</u> you become.
>
> = <u>As</u> you eat more fast food, you become fatter.

 혼공개념 one of the 최상급 + 복수명사

1 의미: 가장 ~한 것들 중 하나

> 예 He is <u>one of the most legendary rappers</u> in the world.
>
> *Frozen* is <u>one of the most successful animation movies</u>.

Ⓐ 다음 빈칸에 들어갈 단어를 쓰시오. 주어진 단어가 있을 경우 반드시 그 단어의 형태를 바꾸어 쓰시오.

① A: _____ season do you like more, summer _____ winter?
B: I like winter _____ because I was born in Toronto.

② A: _____ do you _____, bus _____ train?
B: I prefer a train _____ it makes fewer stops.

③ The _____ medicine tastes, the more it works. (bad)

④ The more fast food you eat, the _____ you become. (fat)
= _____ you eat more fast food, you become fatter.

Ⓑ 다음 문장이 최상급의 의미를 가지도록 밑줄 친 부분을 어법에 맞게 고치시오.

① He is one of the <u>more legendary rappers</u> in the world.
_____

② *Frozen* is one of <u>the most successful animation movie</u>.
_____

③ Busan is one of <u>the large city</u> in South Korea.
_____

④ Jun is one of <u>the most patient person</u>.
_____

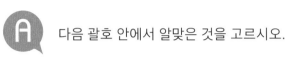

A 다음 괄호 안에서 알맞은 것을 고르시오.

① Which is (more / most) interesting, history or math?

② Which (food / dessert) do you prefer, bulgogi (or / and) bibimbap?

③ The (more / less) consumers buy, the lower the prices go.

④ This is one of (better / the best) articles you've written so far.

B 우리말과 일치하도록 주어진 표현들을 올바르게 배열하시오.

① 녹색과 파란색 중 어떤 색깔을 더 좋아하니?
(prefer / or / which / do / color / you / green / blue)?

_____

② 그는 반에서 가장 수줍음 많은 학생 중 하나이다.
(is / he / of / one / students / shyest / in his class / the)

_____

③ 당신이 더 많이 운동할수록, 당신의 몸은 더 강해진다.
(the stronger / the more / you / becomes / work out / your body)

_____

C 다음은 Kevin의 보고서이다. 우리말을 참고하여 빈칸을 적절한 영어 표현으로 채우시오.

> I think a cheetah is ① <u>세상에서 가장 빠른 동물 중 하나이다</u>. It is ② <u>사람</u>
> <u>보다 훨씬 빠르다</u>.

① one of _____ in the world

② _____ than humans

A. 다음 문장이 최상급의 의미를 가지도록 밑줄 친 부분을 어법에 맞게 고치시오.

① He is one of the <u>more legendary rappers</u> in the world.

_____

② *Frozen* is one of <u>the most successful animation movie</u>.

_____

③ Busan is one of <u>the large city</u> in South Korea.

_____

B. 다음 괄호 안에서 알맞은 것을 고르시오.

④ Which (food / dessert) do you prefer, bulgogi (or / and) bibimbap?

⑤ The (more / less) consumers buy, the lower the prices go.

C. 우리말과 일치하도록 주어진 표현들을 올바르게 배열하시오.

⑥ 녹색과 파란색 중 어떤 색깔을 더 좋아하니?

(prefer / or / which / do / color / you / green / blue)?

_____

⑦ 당신이 더 많이 운동할수록, 당신의 몸은 더 강해진다.

(the stronger / the more / you / becomes / work out / your body)

_____

정답 ① most legendary rappers ② the most successful animation movies ③ the largest cities ④ food, or ⑤ more ⑥ Which color do you prefer, green or blue? ⑦ The more you work out, the stronger your body becomes.

명사절을 이끄는 접속사

혼공개념 접속사 that이란?

1 접속사 that: 뒤에 따라오는 문장을 하나의 단어처럼 포장해주는 역할을 함

예 That he cheated on the test was true.(주어)

= It was true that he cheated on the test.

I don't think (that) he will make it on time.(목적어)

My strength is that I trust myself.(보어)

The belief that practice makes perfect was right.(동격)

* hope, belief, idea, fact와 같이 추상적 단어 뒤에 주로 쓰임

혼공 팁

시간, 조건을 나타내는 접속사(when, if, until...) 이끄는 부사절에서는 미래 시제 대신 현재를 쓴다.

예 If he makes it on time, everybody will be satisfied.

혼공개념 접속사 if VS whether

1 접속사 if와 whether: '~인지'의 의미로 쓰이며 뒤에 따라오는 문장을 하나의 단어처럼 포상해수는 역할을 함

2 위치: whether는 주어, 목적어, 보어 자리에 다 오는 것이 가능하지만, if는 주어 자리에 올 수 없고, 목적어를 이끄는 명사절에서만 whether를 대체할 수 있음

예 Whether he will come or not is not important.

= It is not important whether he will come or not.

I don't know whether(if) they have different ideas.

혼공 연습

A 다음 밑줄 친 접속사가 이끄는 절의 역할을 주어, 목적어, 보어, 동격 중에서 골라 적으시오.

① My strength is <u>that</u> I trust myself.

_____

② I don't think <u>that</u> he will make it on time.

_____

③ The belief <u>that</u> practice makes perfect was right.

_____

④ It was true <u>that</u> he cheated on the test.

_____

⑤ It is not important <u>whether</u> he will come or not.

_____

B 다음 밑줄 친 부분을 어법에 맞게 고치시오.

① If he <u>will make</u> it on time, everybody will be satisfied.

_____

② <u>If</u> he will come or not is not important.

_____

③ My strength is <u>which</u> I trust myself.

_____

A 다음 괄호 안에서 어법상 알맞은 단어를 고르시오.

① I wonder (if / that) Sarah trusts me.

② We didn't realize (if / that) Jun was interested in science.

③ It is true (if / that) some volcanoes in Hawaii erupted recently.

④ (If / Whether) she will leave her country depends on her dad's decision.

B 다음 if의 쓰임이 같으면 O, 다르면 X를 쓰시오.

① You can go out and play if it is sunny in the afternoon.
   I doubted if he could pass the driving test. _____

② If you are not busy, please help me with my homework.
   Go and see if the machine is working. _____

C 우리말과 일치하도록 빈칸에 알맞은 단어를 쓰시오.

① Mr. Park은 그가 심각한 실수를 했다는 사실을 숨겼다.

   Mr. Park hid the fact _____ he had made a serious mistake.

② 나는 그가 위대한 작곡가가 될 운명을 타고 났다고 믿는다.

   I believe _____ he was born to be a great composer.

③ 당신이 그 제안을 받아들일지가 중요하다.

   _____ you will accept the offer is important.

A. 다음 밑줄 친 접속사가 이끄는 절의 역할을 주어, 목적어, 보어, 동격 중에서 골라 적으시오.

① My strength is <u>that</u> I trust myself.　　　　　　　　_____

② I don't think <u>that</u> he will make it on time.　　　　　_____

③ The belief <u>that</u> practice makes perfect was right.　　_____

④ It is not important <u>whether</u> he will come or not.　　_____

B. 다음 괄호 안에서 어법상 알맞은 단어를 고르시오.

⑤ I wonder (if / that) Sarah trusts me.

⑥ We didn't realize (if / that) Jun was interested in science.

⑦ It is true (if / that) some volcanoes in Hawaii erupted recently.

⑧ (If / Whether) she will leave her country depends on her dad's decision.

C. 우리말과 일치하도록 빈칸에 알맞은 단어를 쓰시오.

⑨ 나는 그가 위대한 작곡가가 될 운명을 타고 났다고 믿는다.

　　I believe _____ he was born to be a great composer.

⑩ 당신이 그 제안을 받아들일지가 중요하다.

　　_____ you will accept the offer is important.

정답 ① 보어 ② 목적어 ③ 동격 ④ 주어 ⑤ if ⑥ that ⑦ that ⑧ Whether ⑨ that ⑩ Whether

부사절을 이끄는 접속사

 혼공개념 시간을 나타내는 접속사

1 while(~하는 동안에), when / as(~할 때), since(~이후로)

> 예) While you are swimming, I'll go out and buy something to eat.
>
> When(As) I walked down the street, I saw a cute puppy.
>
> Since I was 19, I've been meeting a lot of foreigners.

혼공개념 이유를 나타내는 접속사

1 because / since / as(~ 때문에)

> 예) Since it was dark, I couldn't see the thief.
>
> John may need some help as he has never done that.

혼공개념 양보를 나타내는 접속사

1 although / though(~에도 불구하고)

> 예) (Al)though the weather was bad, we went on a picnic.

혼공개념 조건을 나타내는 접속사

1 if(만약 ~한다면), unless(만약 ~가 아니라면)

> 예) If he comes with you, I won't go to the party.
>
> Unless you are good at English, it will be difficult to do.
>
> = If you are not good at English, it will be difficult to do.

A 다음 빈칸에 해당하는 알맞은 접속사를 쓰시오.

시간을 나타내는 접속사	이유를 나타내는 접속사
양보를 나타내는 접속사	조건을 나타내는 접속사

β 다음 빈칸에 들어갈 알맞은 접속사를 쓰시오.

① _____ you are swimming, I'll go out and buy something to eat.(~하는 동안에)

② W_____ I walked down the street, I saw a cute puppy.(~할 때)

③ _____ I was 19, I've been meeting a lot of foreigners.(~이후로)

④ S_____ it was dark, I couldn't see the thief.(~ 때문에)

⑤ John may need some help a_____ he has never done that.(~ 때문에)

⑥ _____ the weather was bad, we went on a picnic.(~에도 불구하고)

⑦ _____ he comes with you, I won't go to the party.(만약 ~한다면)

⑧ _____ you are good at English, it will be difficult to do.(만약 ~가 아니라면)

= _____ you are _____ good at English, it will be difficult to do.

A 다음 괄호 안에서 알맞은 접속사를 고르시오.

① (Because / Though) I didn't like the food, I had to try some.

② I won't go outside (if / unless) it gets sunny.

③ (Since / Although) Jane was honest, they wouldn't listen to her.

④ Jason called me (while / since) I was taking a shower.

⑤ She might fail the test (unless / because) she studies harder.

B 밑줄 친 접속사의 쓰임이 자연스러우면 O, 그렇지 않으면 X 표시하고 올바르게 고치시오.

① I fell asleep <u>while</u> I was writing an essay in my room.   _____

② <u>As</u> he doesn't work out regularly, he stays healthy.   _____

③ <u>When</u> I was 23, I have written a lot of stories.   _____

C 다음 사진을 보고, 괄호 안의 단어를 이용하여 영작하시오.

_____, she can eat a lot. (thin)

A. 다음 빈칸에 해당하는 알맞은 접속사를 쓰시오.

시간을 나타내는 접속사	이유를 나타내는 접속사
양보를 나타내는 접속사	조건을 나타내는 접속사

B. 다음 빈칸에 들어갈 알맞은 접속사를 쓰시오.

① S_____ it was dark, I couldn't see the thief.(~ 때문에)

② John may need some help a_____ he has never done that.(~ 때문에)

③ _____ the weather was bad, we went on a picnic.(~에도 불구하고)

④ _____ you are good at English, it is difficult to do.(만약 ~가 아니라면)

C. 다음 괄호 안에서 알맞은 접속사를 고르시오.

⑤ (Because / Though) I didn't like the food, I had to try some.

⑥ I won't go outside (if / unless) it gets sunny.

⑦ (Since / Although) Jane was honest, they wouldn't listen to her.

혼공 기초 영문법
LEVEL 3
정답

01 to부정사 심화 1

Part 1

A ① for Jun, It is very difficult ˇto concentrate in the morning. ② for her, The box is too heavyˇto carry. ③ for him, It was impossibleˇto work with his father. ④ of them, It is so nice toˇ say so.

B for 목적격: hard, difficult, possible, impossible, important, dangerous

of 목적격: nice, kind, brave, polite, foolish, careless, rude, stupid

Part 2

A ① of ② of ③ of ④ for

B ① for him ② of them ③ for us

C ① It was difficult for me to understand his class. ② It is easy for Jun to solve this math problem.

 ## 02 to부정사 심화 2

Part 1

A ① He decidedˇto go on a business trip. ② My mom told me ˇto be late again. ③ My brother told meˇto turn off the TV. ④ Kevin's mom told Kevinˇto leave the water running.

B ① 공부하기 위해 ② 듣게 되어서 ③ 돕다니 ④ 앉기에 ⑤ 되었다

Part 2

A ① My sister told me not to wear her clothes. ② My mom wanted me not to play computer games too often. ③ Jason advised us not to walk around while we eat.

B ① have (some coffee) ② call (Mr. Kim)

C ① 유명해졌다 ② 체중을 감량하기 위해 ③ 입기에

 ## 03 to부정사 심화 3

Part 1

A ① are to catch, 잡으려면 ② was to be seen, 보이지 않았다 ③ were never to see, 결코 볼 운명이 아니었다 ④ are to wash, 씻어야 한다 ⑤ are to visit, 방문할 예정이다

B ① 명사적 용법 ② be to 용법 ③ be to 용법 ④ 명사적 용법

Part 2

A ① are to obey ② are to go out for a walk

B ① John is to marry Sally next month. ② You are to finish the project by this Friday. ③ She was never to see her family again.

 ## 04 to부정사 심화 4

Part 1

A 본문 23쪽 표를 참고하세요.

B ① is about to start ② seemed to like ③ pretended not to know ④ are ready to fight ⑤ happened to meet him

Part 2

A ① pretended ② manage ③ supposed ④ eager

B ① The bus is about to leave. ② The soccer player was willing to help the poor. ③ Jun happened to meet Jason on the street.

 ## 05 동명사 / to부정사를 좋아하는 동사

Part 1

A ① enjoy, finish, quit, mind, give up, avoid ② choose, wish, want, expect, plan, decide ③ hate, begin, start, like, love ④ try, stop, forget, remember, regret

B ① playing ② going ③ to be ④ to see ⑤ raining, to rain ⑥ locking, to lock ⑦ sending, to send ⑧ talking, to talk

Part 2

A ① reading the novel ② to sell the car ③ to play with those children 또는 playing with those children

B ① I couldn't remember meeting Tom last week. ② My father finally gave up smoking.

C to clean my room

 ## 06 동명사 관용 구문

Part 1

A 본문 31쪽 표를 참고하세요.

B ① have, having ② meet, meeting ③ clean, cleaning ④ buy, buying ⑤ get, getting ⑥ read, reading

Part 2

A ① meeting ② eating ③ listening ④ help ⑤ telling

B ① She felt like crying. ② Mom was busy cooking in the kitchen. ③ The police officer couldn't help wondering what he was doing.

현재분사/과거분사

Part 1

A ① sleeping ② fallen ③ broken ④ locked

B ① running ② used ③ barking

C ① painted ② playing ③ standing

Part 2

A ① hiding → hidden ② speaking → spoken ③ escape → escaped

B ① painted by Jessy will be sold ② is the boy playing baseball over there ③ talk with the man standing behind the tree ④ He collected the fallen leaves ⑤ The girl playing the violin is my sister

 분사구문 1

Part 1

A ① Walking home ② Seeing me on the street ③ Being tired

B ① you turn to the left ② Though she was sick

C ① Arriving at the hotel ② Listening to music

Part 2

A ① As ② When

B ① Open → Opening ② Get up → Getting up

C ① Since he was thirsty ② Because he was raised in England

 분사구문 2

Part 1

A ① Not knowing her name ② Not sleeping well last night ③ Not being good at math

B ① The weather being good ② The store being closed ③ Having studied English in Canada

Part 2

A ① It being cold ② Being young ③ The weather being fine

B ① Not having saved enough money ② Having finished reading the report ③ Having been raised in China

 관계대명사 심화 1

Part 1

A ① which ② who ③ which ④ that

B ① I met a girl whose dream is to be a traveller. ② The building whose design I love is amazing. ③ Tom was a businessman whose mom was a teacher. ④ I know a boy whose brother is a singer.

C 본문 47쪽 표를 참고하세요.

Part 2

A ① who is a doctor ② whose son was crying ③ that I found difficult to learn

B ① who is talking on the phone ② that I bought yesterday ③ whose name is Nancy

C ① whose → which(that) ② which → who(that)

 관계대명사 심화 2

Part 1

A ① that, 이것은 내가 지금껏 들었던 가장 아름다운 음악이다. ② what, 그는 그녀에게 그녀가 필요로 했던 것을 주었다. ③ that, 그는 그가 벌었던 모든 돈을 써버렸다. ④ that, 우리쪽으로 걸어오고 있는 소년과 그의 개를 봐라. ⑤ that, 그는 우리 반에서 러시아어를 할 수 있는 유일한 학생이다. ⑥ what, 그가 말했던 것을 이해했니?

Part 2

A ① This is the only palace that was built during the Baekje Dynasty. ② I remembered something that my grandfather had said. ③ The only problem that we have is time.

B ① Did you hear what our principal said? ② My mom gave me what I really wanted to buy. ③ I can tell you what she talked about.

C ① What Tom wants her to do ② What interested me

 관계부사

Part 1

A ① January is the month when it is really cold. ② That is the reason why he is always late. ③ New York is the city where I lived when I was seven years old. ④ This is the store where I bought the shampoo. ⑤ Gimhae is the city where I was born. ⑥ This is the way(how) he fixes a computer easily.

A ① when ② which ③ where ④ that

B ① ⓑ ② ⓒ ③ ⓐ

C ① where Jun was born ② why we have to work out regularly ③ where you met John

 13 관계사의 계속적 용법

Part 1

A ① where ② where ③ where ④ why ⑤ where

B ① who lived a happy life ② and there she studied architecture ③ and they became doctors

Part 2

A ① where ② when

B ① when ② when ③ where

C ① which was bad news ② which lasts about two months

 14 상관접속사

Part 1

A 본문 63쪽 표를 참고하세요.

B ① like ② have ③ was ④ is ⑤ were ⑥ is ⑦ intelligent

Part 2

A ① Both ② Either ③ but ④ Neither

B ① Not you but he has ② eat now or eat after the concert ③ Erasers as well pencils are

C ① has ② were ③ are

 15 과거완료

Part 1

A ① had, gone ② had, been ③ had, seen ④ had, lost

B ① 2, 1 ② 2, 1 ③ 1, 2 ④ 1, 2

Part 2

A ① the bus had already left ② I had had lunch with him once ③ It hadn't(had not) been cleaned

B ① had already taken ② had already left

C her, money, had, saved

 16 수일치

Part 1

A ① is ② is ③ is ④ is ⑤ are ⑥ is ⑦ is ⑧ is

B ① are ② were ③ has ④ was ⑤ were

Part 2

A ① means ② makes ③ is

B ① apple, was ② apples, were

C ① the students like English ② rich save money ③ The number of students, (has) increased

 17 시제 일치와 예외

Part 1

A ① were ② are ③ will be ④ were ⑤ had bought ⑥ would get

B ① goes ② is ③ boils ④ is ⑤ discovered ⑥ invented

Part 2

A ① goes ② promised, would buy ③ rises

B ① would ② would ③ moves

 18 기타 조동사

Part 1

A 본문 79쪽 표를 참고하세요.

B ① stayed → stay ② was → be ③ fishing → fish ④ played → play

C ① get ② getting ③ be ④ cure

Part 2

A ① used to ② had better ③ would like to ④ would rather

B ① had better not go swimming ② to raise a few hamsters at home

C to be a palace

 19 조동사 + have + p.p.

Part 1

A ① must have been ② must have finished ③ should have been ④ should have gone ⑤ may have forgotten

B ① could have ② can't(cannot) have ③ should have ④ must have ⑤ may(might) have

Part 2

A ① must have stayed ② should have flushed ③ can't (cannot) have met ④ may(might) have been

B ① should ② can't ③ should

C must have slept, should have studied

20 현재완료 진행형 / 수동태

Part 1

A ① He has repaired the car. ② He has been repairing the car. ③ The problems have been solved. ④ He has been chosen as a leader. ⑤ A new building has been built by the company.

B ① repairing ② solved ③ chosen ④ built

C ① waited → waiting ② worked → working ③ destroying → destroyed

Part 2

A ① has been reading ② has been repairing(fixing) ③ have been talking

B ① has been watching, since ② has been crying, hours ③ has been fixed(repaired)

C have been studying, 00 years

21 조동사 + be + p.p.

Part 1

A ① Your job must be done by 1 p.m. ② The full moon can be seen in my yard. ③ This puzzle will be solved by a famous professor. ④ All of my classmates will be invited to my birthday party.

B ① to ② for ③ by ④ as

C ① Our room was filled with smoke. ② My parents were satisfied with my test score. ③ We were surprised at the news.

Part 2

A ① be saved ② be seen ③ be discussed ④ be done ⑤ be handed in ⑥ be planted

B ① to ② for ③ as ④ by

C ① interested in ② married to ③ was full of(was filled with)

22 화법 전환

Part 1

A ① 간접 ② 직접 ③ 간접 ④ 직접

B ① she, needed ② told, she, would, me ③ asked, my, was ④ if(whether), knew ⑤ to, study ⑥ suggested, should

Part 2

A ① said, said, she, was ② said, told, she, didn't, like ③ said, said, they, wanted

B ① to ② shouted ③ told ④ not to

C I → he

23 가정법 과거

Part 1

A ① were ② were ③ were

B ① were, wouldn't go ② had, could buy ③ were, could fly ④ won, would go

C ① told, would(could) ② weren't(were not)

Part 2

A ① would(could) go ② would(could) donate

B ① were, wouldn't, ask ② lived, would

C ① If it were not cold(= were warm) outside, we could go on a picnic. ② If I had a camera, I could take a picture of you.

24 가정법 과거완료

Part 1

A ① had been diligent, would have hired ② had been a bird, could have flown ③ had studied harder, could have been

B ① is, will ② were, would ③ had been, would have hired

C ① had brought, wouldn't have ② hadn't made, have won ③ had gotten up, could have caught

Part 2

A ① had known ② had been ③ have seen ④ have told

B ① I would have given them something to drink ② he could have won the race ③ I had not been tired

C ① had eaten, wouldn't have ② had studied, failed

25 I wish 가정법

Part 1

A ① I wish I were taller than you. ② I wish I had got(gotten) super powers. ③ I wish I had been rich. ④ I wish I had spoken French fluently.

B ① were ② had been ③ spoke ④ had spoken

C ① had been taller than her ② had won the contest

Part 2

A ① had ② had done ③ hadn't rained

B ① were ② had traveled ③ had lived

C ① baked some cookies ② had won

 26 as if 가정법

Part 1

A ① were ② had watched ③ is not ④ didn't meet

B ① had been ② talks, were ③ talks, had met ④ talks, he had been

Part 2

A ① were not ② had seen ③ had happened

B ① talks, he, were ② talks, were ③ hadn't, slept

 27 최상급의 표현

Part 1

A ① the tallest ② (the) fastest ③ the most important

B ① city ② more ③ than ④ things ⑤ than ⑥ teacher was

Part 2

A ① as ② than ③ most ④ better ⑤ student is

B ① the most popular ② energetic as ③ talkative as

C ① No other way is more expensive than this. ② Nothing was as bad as this disaster. ③ The Pacific Ocean is the largest ocean in the world.

 28 비교급/최상급의 관용 표현

Part 1

A ① Which, or, more ② Which, prefer, or, because ③ worse ④ fatter, As

B ① most legendary rappers ② the most successful animation movies ③ the largest cities ④ the most patient persons (people)

Part 2

A ① more ② food, or ③ more ④ the best

B ① Which color do you prefer, green or blue? ② He is one of the shyest students in his class. ③ The more you work out, the stronger your body becomes.

C ① the fastest animals ② much faster

 29 명사절을 이끄는 접속사

Part 1

A ① 보어 ② 목적어 ③ 동격 ④ 주어 ⑤ 주어

B ① makes ② Whether ③ that

Part 2

A ① if ② that ③ that ④ Whether

B ① X ② X

C ① that ② that ③ Whether

 30 부사절을 이끄는 접속사

Part 1

A 시간을 나타내는 접속사: while, when, as, since
이유를 나타내는 접속사: because, since, as
양보를 나타내는 접속사: although, though
조건을 나타내는 접속사: if, unless

B ① While ② When ③ Since ④ Since ⑤ as ⑥ Though (Although) ⑦ If ⑧ Unless, If, not

Part 2

A ① Though ② unless ③ Although ④ while ⑤ unless

B ① O ② X, Though(Although) ③ X, Since

C Though(Although) she is(looks) thin